More Praise for
Lead Generation for the Complex Sale

"Brian Carroll 'gets' that marketing and sales must have a common definition of a lead and a 'sales ready' lead is a targeted decision maker who is curious how you have helped someone with the same job title in the same industry achieve a goal or solve a problem."

> —Mike Bosworth, author *Solution Selling* and coauthor *CustomerCentric Selling*

"The lead generation game has changed in the age of the Internet; if you don't have this new playbook your competitors will. Brian Carroll closes the loop on lead generation, taking you from defining a lead, thinking like your prospects, tactics to increase lead generation, passing leads from marketing to sales, measuring the results, and nurturing the leads for increased revenue. If you don't read and then apply lessons from *Lead Generation for the Complex Sale,* then let me know how things work out for you."

> —Bryan Eisenberg, *New York Times* and *Wall Street Journal* bestselling author of *Call To Action*

"Great book on a very important topic. The author speaks from a true knowledge-base and offers a 'Soup-to-Nuts' instruction of principles, strategies, and tactics from which the reader can greatly profit."

> —Bob Burg, author of *Endless Referrals: Network Your Everyday Contacts into Sales*

"Great book! I heartily recommend *Lead Generation for the Complex Sale* because it's packed with practical, hands-on advice. In particular, Chapter 3 'Defining Your Best Lead' should be required reading for CSOs and CMOs alike *before* you invest in any more demand generation campaigns!"

> —Anne Holland, Publisher, MarketingSherpa Inc.

"Brian Carroll has unveiled some of the most guarded secrets of lead generation experts. His approach to generating leads for the complex sale is not only on-target but will produce results as well."

> —John M. Coe, President, Sales & Marketing Institute

"It's never been tougher to crack into corporate accounts. To help your sales force, create a lead generation program based on the multiple strategies in this information-rich book. In today's crazy market, it's the best way to slash your sales cycle."

> —Jill Konrath, Chief Sales Officer, author of *Selling to Big Companies*

"Brian Carroll has written a no-nonsense, practical guide to sales lead generation that will help anybody who is looking for advice based on real-world experience. He makes the case for a strong working relationship between the sales and marketing functions."

> —Ruth P. Stevens, President, eMarketing Strategy, and author of *Trade Show and Event Marketing*

"Brian Carroll gives us insightful lessons in the complete sales lead management process, including the critical organizational issues that will determine success or failure. Read it, and start putting Brian's advice to work immediately."

> —Bob Donath, Bob Donath & Co., marketing author and consultant

"Does your company have an uncrossable abyss between your sales and marketing functions? If so, then this book will help you bridge that gap and fill the void. If you follow a few of its simple concepts you will be able to drive significantly enhanced sales and marketing effectiveness."

> —Guy R. Powell, DemandROMI—Prove and Improve your Marketing Performance, author, *Return on Marketing Investment*

"Brian's book is an absolute must read for any B-to-B marketers."

> —Russell Kern, President, The Kern Organization

"Brian tackles a tough subject and gives it the depth it deserves. Anyone selling a complex product or service will avoid the common mistakes and close more sales if they follow the advice in this book."

> —Kristin Zhivago, author of *Rivers of Revenue*

"Finally, a book that addresses the realities of today's selling environment. Brian Carroll has broken new ground in this comprehensive, utterly practical, and thoughtful guide to sales lead generation."

> —Michael W. McLaughlin, coauthor of *Guerrilla Marketing for Consultants*

"Trade shows are hard work for an individual and expensive for a firm. Most shows are geared to complex sales—i.e., you are selling on the floor—so this book is a definitive resource in how to develop the structure of a lead, the rationale for a lead, and the importance of follow-up. If marketing and sales do not understand these three components, you are doomed at a trade show. Working together will improve the quality of both marketing and sales—and make everybody happier."

    —Julia O'Connor, President of TradeShowTraining.com

"The quality and quantity of leads does as much to determine sales success as face-to-face selling prowess, yet little has been written about lead generation. This book fills the void. Carroll really understands lead generation."

    —Ford Harding, author of *Creating Rainmakers*, Harding & Company

"A logical and straightforward methodology to maximize your likelihood of success. A good primer for the uninitiated and a great refresher for the experienced."

    —Bill Herr, Managing Director, sales lead development programs, CMP Media, LLC

"This book should be a must read for all people involved in the sales and marketing process. Definitely one for your business book collection."

    —Bob Freytag, President, Introworks Branding and Marketing Communications

"Brian masterfully tackles the single biggest issue for enterprise marketing today."

    —John Neeson, Managing Director & Cofounder, SiriusDecisions Inc.

"This book is essential reading for anyone in marketing today. It will make a difference in your company's lead generation results!"

    —Dan Kosch & Mark Shonka, copresidents of IMPAX Corporation and coauthors of the best-selling book *Beyond Selling Value*

"If *Lead Generation for the Complex Sale* helps your business grow half as fast as Brian Carroll's has, it may be the best marketing and sales investment you make all year."

    — Keith Ferrazzi, CEO of sales consulting and training firm Ferrazzi Greenlight and former CMO of Starwood Hotels and Deloitte Consulting

"Exhaustive coverage and discussion of the lead generation modalities and the synergies therein, ranging from the classical modes such as telemarketing and direct mail through such new generation modes as blogs and podcasts, is insightful. A very compelling read indeed."
　　—Sharmila C. Chatterjee, Visiting Professor, MIT

"The time has come for sales and marketing teams to finally unite to create and solidify customer relationships. This book provides sound execution strategies for collaboration that leads to results."
　　—Barbara Geraghty, President, Visionary Selling

"*Lead Generation for the Complex Sale* is an important and intelligent addition to the small but growing body of literature on business-to-business sales lead generation."
　　—Bob Bly, author, *The Copywriter's Handbook*

"Chapter six alone is worth the price of the book. If you're puzzled about the nuts and bolts of building a lead-gen plan that actually works, you're in luck. It's right here."
　　—Chris Coleman, speaker, author and cofounder, greenbananaproject.com

Lead Generation for the COMPLEX SALE

Boost the Quality and Quantity of Leads to Increase Your ROI

Brian J. Carroll

McGraw-Hill

New York Chicago San Francisco Lisbon London
Madrid Mexico City Milan New Delhi San Juan
Seoul Singapore Sydney Toronto

The _McGraw-Hill_ Companies

4 5 6 7 8 9 0 DOC/DOC 0 9 8

ISBN 0-07-145897-2

This publication is designed to provide accurate and authoritative information in regard to the subject matter covered. It is sold with the understanding that neither the author nor the publisher is engaged in rendering legal, accounting, or other professional service. If legal advice or other expert assistance is required, the services of a competent professional person should be sought.

—From a Declaration of Principles jointly adopted by Committee of the American Bar Association and a Committee of Publishers.

McGraw-Hill books are available at special quantity discounts to use as premiums and sales promotions, or for use in corporate training programs. For more information, please write to the Director of Special Sales, McGraw-Hill Professional, Two Penn Plaza, New York, NY 10121-2298. Or contact your local bookstore.

Contents

Acknowledgments

To give credit where credit is due, I would be remiss if I did not express my gratitude to those without whose constant support this book would not exist. To wife Mindy and children Madalynn and Abigale for your love and patience. To contributing editors Brandon Stamschror and Pat Lorch and editors Donya Dickerson, Mindy Carroll, and Sandra Carroll for helping see this through. To business partners Brandon Stamschror, Michelle Passe, Nikki Lorch, and Pat Lorch for the encouragement that this could become reality. To Mom and Dad for nurturing my love of learning and for your inspiration. To all of my friends and colleagues, especially Jill Konrath and John Coe, who have contributed to the development of this book. To our clients for enabling our growth. And to God for making it all so. Thank you!

Introduction

Keeping the pipeline full of qualified leads is vitally important in today's challenging business climate, so important, in fact, that consistent lead generation is often imperative to a company's very survival. Add to the equation that *your* sale always seems to be more complex than most, and the challenge becomes downright daunting, doesn't it?

Exactly what is a complex sale? It is associated with businesses that are engaged in long-term sales processes that require prolonged education and nurturing of the prospect, frequently over a 6- to 36-month sales cycle. Companies that use the complex sale provide solutions to their clients that tend to be sophisticated, designed to solve crucial business issues, and are managed deliberately and with precision. Ultimately, these solutions can require significant investment of dollars and the buy-in of the company's senior management. The complex sale most often manifests itself in the business-to-business environment, though it is not always limited to that sector.

Because of the unique demands of the complex sale, lead generation has become a major roadblock for marketers as they spin their wheels looking for strategies and tactics that can consistently and measurably push the sales needle forward.

Why is lead generation inherently more challenging in the complex sale?

- **Fewer opportunities:** Although the deal value of each sale is extremely high, there are simply fewer opportunities as compared to more transactional selling environments. More attention therefore must be paid to identifying those relatively few and valuable opportunities.

- **Commoditization is more difficult to overcome:** Marketers must work much more diligently and creatively to differentiate their organizations from increasing competition. Exposure is not enough; there must be a value proposition that resonates with prospects.
- **Increased selling at the executive level:** There must be a more intelligent and varied approach to reaching and converting executives who are more often the economic buyers for complex solutions.
- **Must reach the sphere of influence:** Buying processes frequently involve a team approach. Enlisting the support of one decision maker is rarely enough. The sphere of influence must be identified and a targeted, multipronged approach taken to reach as many as possible.
- **Less selling time:** Because of longer sales cycles, salespeople cannot afford to spend time on unqualified leads. They must focus attention on opportunities that have the greatest likelihood of closing.
- **Return on investment:** Direct return from lead generation activity takes time to surface. A solid plan for reporting and measuring reliable indicators must be in place to justify continued investment.

At my company, we wonder, how did it get to be like this? The scope and complexity of the business of lead generation have grown enormously since we began as a teleprospecting firm in 1995, and we occasionally just have to step back and exclaim, "wow."

In all respects, there was a time that carrying on a conversation was much easier than it is now, and that is no more evident than in the marketplace. It used to be easier to talk with high-level executives because there simply were not as many barriers to beginning the conversation.

A shift that marked the increasing difficulty in reaching people became apparent in the early 1990s. To those of us involved in producing leads for salespeople back then, calling the prospect on the phone with a short pitch more often than not initiated a conversation leading to an appointment. Advances in technology have made that a thing of the past. The objectives of good dialogue and conversation have not changed, but the ways of winning the complex sale today are decidedly different.

The Internet, e-mail, and voice mail had not yet begun to revolutionize communication. Most companies didn't use voice mail or e-mail to any great extent, and the Internet was just moving beyond its limited university campus profile. Caller ID didn't exist on most corporate phone systems. A letter posted by mail was ordinarily the most effective way of communicating on business matters, and the fax machine was the only rapid means of communication. Executive assistants were the primary point of access.

The practice of selling became more complex as the business climate evolved, in many ways spurred by the burgeoning communications technologies. It became apparent to us that a formal lead generation discipline was very much in order, particularly in light of the changing face of sales and marketing for the complex sale. Our exposure dictated that an intelligent, sophisticated, multimodal, integrated solution would be needed if lead generation was going to be effective going forward. No more cookie-cutter tactics; we were seeing technologies that would give us the ability to tailor and personalize our reach, and there began the results that have made lead generation what it is today.

So, plain and simply, the purpose of this book is to help marketers and corporate leaders assemble the necessary tools to more confidently develop customer relationships—with the importance of business-to-business lead generation for the complex sale always in mind. Our approach is a holistic one that recognizes that lead generation must include sales and marketing efforts that work together in harmony towards the common end. It dispels common myths and provides proven strategies and tactics that can be replicated and implemented immediately in the interest of developing new customers and improving your return on investment (ROI).

Most of what I say in this book deals with companies that have a direct sales force. Generally, these principles also hold true for those with a sales channel or those who sell through partners or channels. Regardless of sales structure, experience dictates that the complex sale more often than not entails a *consultative* approach to selling.

A mind-set that is consultative starts well before opportunities are handed over to sales. It is a long-term process that engages targeted prospects as early in the buying process as possible, and it does not relegate to the garbage bin those not ready to buy yet. A well-conceived plan that keeps the lead generation vehicle on track is necessary.

Consider that a cross-country trip requires the aid of both itinerary and map to arrive on time. Without proper planning and direction, you tend to get lost, wander aimlessly, likely take a lot of different side roads, or end up traveling the same old routes. So, too, for lead generation. And frequently with the same unsatisfactory results. My hope is that this book can become your road map, in a direct and timely way, for customizing your own plan for achieving a successful lead generation program that will bring you new customers and accelerate your growth rate.

Lead Generation
for the
COMPLEX
SALE

Part One

Fundamentals of Lead Generation for the Complex Sale

Chapter One

Essential Lead Generation

Not Like it Used to Be

It wasn't long ago that lead generation campaigns were largely based on unfocused direct mail campaigns along with, perhaps, a flashy Web site, sporadic trade show appearances, innumerable e-mail blasts, and on-and-off-again telemarketing campaigns that had little to do with the rest—all with the express hope that somehow, something would work. If this is your lead generation strategy and you are still waiting for results, I'm here to say stop. Studies confirm that response rates for lead generation campaigns of this nature—the old way—just don't work. The course of passive reactivity is of little value in pursuing the complex sale.

The business scene today is rife with new competition. Budgets are shrinking, and marketing and sales teams are stretched to the limit to do more with less.

Many business-to-consumer marketing resources exist, but they are of little relevance in business-to-business where the complex sale, a phenomenon in its own right, requires a holistic approach that considers all of the marketing and selling components on a total, complete, and ongoing basis.

CEOs traditionally feel they aren't getting enough activity at the top of the sales funnel and demand more leads. Any kind of leads will do, it seems, as long as they are *right now*. Marketers, on the other hand, must continually face the exasperation of having too few high-quality leads and are forced to choose immediate tactics over better long-term planning and execution.

Salespeople, in their primary quest for increased sales, operate under the pressure to more effectively utilize their available leads. In either case, the generation of leads today calls for much more than salespeople getting on the phone in an attempt to schedule appointments. Sadly, this is the exercise in futility where a great many talented salespeople still find themselves trapped. In the end, poorly conceived and executed lead generation is a major impediment to growth.

Who Is Responsible for Generating Leads in the Complex Sale?

Unfortunately, the time-honored struggle of sales to get a foot in the door fails miserably in context of the complex sale. To be successful, a carefully crafted, thoroughly researched, and proven lead generation strategy cannot come from sales—any more than should modern salespeople be burdened with the old, worn-out tactic of cold-call prospecting. Salespeople must be enabled to do what they do best—to sell, with leads that have been qualified as sales ready.

In lead generation, the job of the marketing department is to develop leads to match the buyer's readiness to buy and the seller's expectations of selling. Marketing to sales: "We get the leads; you get the sales." Although sales leads can be generated in any number of ways, some better than others, the high-quality, high-value kind so necessary to the complex sale is quite another matter.

Marketing, by virtue of its province, should be responsible for the actual process of lead generation, if not for accountability then for ensuring that the definition of a qualified lead is properly followed and measured. Marketers must have the perspective to know when the lead is sales ready. Marketers can then more effectively manage the lead generation process and be better placed to measure ROI and revenue contribution.

Nevertheless, there are some organizations that for various reasons still place the responsibility of lead creation with the sales sector. While I disagree that this is the most effective way to generate leads, it's important to note that the tenets offered here can be just as valuable in any case.

Let Sales Sell

According to research by SiriusDecisions, during the last five years the average sales cycle has gotten to be 22 percent longer, typically with three more decision makers participating in the buying process.[1] With the reduced administrative support that there seems to be across the board, more of the

1 "SiriusDecisions 2005 Sales and Marketing Benchmarking Study," (Southport, CT: SiriusDecisions 2005).

seller's time must be spent on writing reports, keeping pace with customers, and maintaining paperwork. Experience with clients of my company points to as little as 35 to 40 percent of the sales staff's time being available for actually moving the sales process forward. And because of the multitude of interrelated aspects of the complex sale, the salesperson is often expected to remain involved beyond the buy, and that can go right through implementation and subsequent ongoing service.

Whether to put more money into sales or into marketing is a dilemma faced by many senior executives. Individuals charged with selling a company's products or services would tell you they need more selling time to generate increased revenue, not more sales leads. And the truth of the matter is, there are a number of indicators supporting the contention that they do have too much else to do and not enough time to sell.

In his book *Return on Marketing Investment,* Guy R. Powell notes that "CEOs often wonder, why should I invest in marketing [lead generation] when I can hire more sales people for the same budget and see a measurable increase in revenue?"[2] Contrarily, our research shows, for the complex sale, it is far more effective to support proven salespeople with good lead generation than to hire additional salespeople.

Still, salespeople succeed in spite of it all. They may have to generate their own leads, in one way or another, to meet their revenue and sales targets. They are often compelled to do their own prospecting for leads independent of any corporate marketing programs. Remember, the sales team is either doing selling activities or prospecting activities. It's like a teeter-totter—when prospecting, the teeter-totter is up, and when pursuing a hot deal it is down.

Today, it takes new salespeople, and hence their productivity, longer to get up to speed. Product- and servicewise, companies are in constant flux, and salespeople have more to sell, more to do. Cross-selling and up-selling often suffer. Where does all of this take us? Current business trends show that complex sales products and services are being commoditized faster, margins are eroding, and salespeople have less time to acquire the necessary knowledge to sell properly as trusted consultative advisors to their customers.

In addition, there are many other issues happening that are affecting whether or not a prospect will buy. For example, companies have many more choices that can solve their needs. The time required to get consensus is taking much longer. The status quo—"decision delay"—is increasing. In addition, the sales landscape has gotten much more competitive. Salespeople are

---

2 Guy R. Powell, *Return on Marketing Investment,* (RPI Press: February, 2003).

forced to sell in situations where they are merely column fodder on a potential customer's spreadsheet. In such situations, sales proposals are simply used to justify a vendor selection decision, a determination that already has been made. Unbeknownst to the salespeople, they may even be responding to nothing more than an RFP (request for proposal) coming from association with a well-entrenched competitor.

Sales teams, unfortunately, aren't always equipped for this new paradigm, nor are the company's marketing processes able to adapt. As the complexity increases, so does the challenge of being able to find a clear value proposition. This is why marketing must assume a pivotal role to help the sales team sell. Marketing must now go beyond the sales lead.

For all intents and purposes, lead generation must be looked at to drive more sales. If not, consider it wasted expense, time, and effort. In the traditional sales funnel, the objective is to convert more leads faster. However, an Aberdeen Group study found that salespeople don't necessarily want more leads but rather more selling time with viable opportunities.[3]

Universal Lead Defined

Additionally, a lot of money is squandered every day because companies lack a clear understanding of what a "sales lead" really means. Consequently, they fail to make lead definition a credible facet of their business. There is consensus among numerous sources that sales fails to act on upwards of 80 percent of the leads it gets, an astounding fact if anywhere near accurate. More than likely, that number is so high because most of the leads that sales receive aren't qualified leads or appropriate buyers for what is being sold.

By definition, a universal sales lead is one that has been determined to fit the profile of the ideal customer, has been qualified as sales ready, and spells out the responsibilities and accountabilities of the participants in the program, sales and marketing.

Actually, our own research reveals that only 1 out of every 10 companies operates under a lead definition that both sales and marketing have agreed upon. There is no better catalyst for building ties between sales and marketing—and no better way to generate a greater return on marketing investment—than the premise that everyone knows what a sales lead really and truly means.

Lead generation represents an important marketing investment, and the systematic development of good lead generation is increasingly a strategic

---

3 *Sales Effectiveness: Helping Sales Sell*, (Boston: Aberdeen Group, June 2004).

imperative worldwide. The right culture, strategy, and tactics are required to make this a cost-effective outlay.

It seems that companies have little problem generating inquires, but inquiries as such are rarely useful without an adequate process to qualify them as sales ready and will often promote activity that produces little result.

Chapter 3 provides an in-depth discussion of creating a universal lead definition for the complex sale.

Reaching the Decision Makers

The complex sale requires that salespeople develop relationships within higher levels of management, often top-level executives. It is the job of marketing to pave the way by providing opportunity to develop these relationships. To reach C-level executives, salespeople must have a strategic dialogue that's relevant to the prospects' interests in return on investment and predictable growth for their stakeholders. The paradigm is one that makes the salesperson a trusted advisor who adds value to the proposition, with the goal of increasing the odds of success for both parties.

In this paradigm, salespeople can no longer tout their solutions as simply better, faster, and cheaper and hope to get the attention of these higher-level economic buyers. And for the very same reason, a lead generation program aimed at reaching these same prospects must focus on value propositions that speak directly to the right decision makers at the right time in their buying process.

Why Is Trust So Important?

Economic buyers increasingly avoid talking to salespeople if at all possible. It seems there is a decided lack of trust of salespeople, and, truth told, they just don't want to be sold. A wealth of readily available information from the Internet and other sources delays the need and value of face-to-face contact with the salesperson until later phases of the buying process. And when at last a participant, to be successful the salesperson must earn the recognition of "trusted advisor." It's been said that trusted advisors are 70 percent more likely to come away with a sale.[4] That becomes easier to understand when you consider that people *buy* based on emotion and then *backfill* with logic.

---

4 Susan Mulcahy, "Evaluating the Cost of Sales Calls in Business-to-Business Markets: A study of more than 23,000 businesses," (Washington: Cahners Research, January 2002), p 8.

Trust has become the theme for a new type of marketing. It's about the relationship. In today's commoditized business climate, the thing that sets companies apart is their ability to create and develop relationships. Companies that understand the concept of how to develop trust and follow with specific actions are positioned to grow and prosper as none other. Decision makers will tell you they value the sales interaction that instills trust that the solution will make their professional lives better. To establish the confidence that your company can provide:

- Buyers must be familiar with you, your company, and what you do.
- Buyers must perceive that you and your company are expert in your field.
- Buyers must believe that you and your company understand their specific needs and can solve them.
- Buyers must like you and your company enough to want to work with you.

It is important to view potential customers as unique individuals, and, in pursuit of their trust, it is time well spent getting to know everything you can about what they do and how they think. How do they work? What are their needs? Where do they go for research? Who in fact are they?

Trust comes from respecting where the prospect is in the buying process and, accordingly, selecting the communication tactics that are warranted. With clear understanding of the buying process, you can remain productively visible throughout. Messaging, content, and tactics are then targeted as is appropriate. The right value proposition, delivered via the correct tactics and on a consistent basis, puts timing in your favor. Be cognizant, then, of what needs to be provided at each stage of the buying process, thus enabling a comfortable transition to the next stage when ready.

Matching Your Strategy with Your Customer's Strategy

In *Mastering the Complex Sale*, Jeff Thull notes that salespeople struggle with the complex sale because their customers do not have a clear buying process defined. He advocates that companies help customers develop appropriate criteria with which to make informed decisions.[5] How will your prospects make informed decisions that will be good for you if they don't have the

---

5 Jeff Thull, *Mastering the Complex Sale: How to Compete and Win When the Stakes are High!*, (Wiley, May 2003).

parameters in their buying process? Better they turn to you as a trusted advisor than to uninformed colleagues. Or to the Internet. Or to trade publications. Or, heaven forbid, to your competitors.

Designing around the customer's buying process and all it represents is as critical as it gets in the development of good lead generation. So how is this done? It all starts with the right lead generation strategy.

Successful lead generation is predicated on a firm foundation of strategy. It is getting to be universal, however, that marketers are under extreme pressure to provide more leads *now*, which tends to prompt an errant emphasis on tactics over strategy. CEOs pay great lip service to the concept of marketing strategy, yet the concern remains overriding that there is never enough activity in the sales funnel. Marketers, therefore, doing exactly as they are directed, following orders, under such circumstances don't follow the general truth that only with good strategy come the right tactics. Meanwhile, there isn't much to move the sales needle.

In addition, with the increasing involvement of upper management and in light of today's buying decision processes, it's clear that much of the selling takes place when the salesperson isn't present. The number of individuals brought into the act of buying as defined by the complex sale has increased by three over the past five years. Not only is the average sales cycle longer and more complex, there are more principals tending to the customer's interests. The era of selling to one economic buyer is long gone. Decisions are now consensus-driven, with more stakeholders weighing in on the decision.

Consequently, the lead generation effort must reach beyond one individual buyer. Astute marketers today recognize that there is an entire sphere of influence represented by contacts associated with the economic buyers, e.g., influencers, information gatherers, opinion molders, and an external sphere of influence represented by end-users as illustrated in Figure1-1. All must be addressed with equal intensity. The more you reach, the better.

Marketers are charged with the responsibility of measuring, identifying, and optimizing performance. The complex sale means working within your prospect's corporate structure. A recent visit to a company revealed a CEO, a sales manager, and a marketing director with altogether divergent views on who was responsible for what. It was quickly apparent that each represented an important target to be reached and influenced equally.

A sign of the times is that no one seems to feel compelled anymore to make decisions without consensus. Perhaps a bit paradoxically, companies seem bent on doing more with less, and if that puts you in the position of failing to reach the right individual at the right time, then no one's purposes

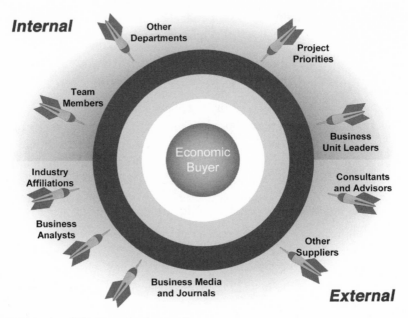

Figure 1-1   Spheres of influence[6]

are served well, yours or the prospect's. Exactly who is that person? Do your homework and then go for the broadest potential group to increase the odds that you are reaching someone who can make the final decision.

"All of Them"

A client's CEO asks his marketing manager, "What are our most effective tactics for generating leads?" The marketer's reply: "All of them."

What? Well, simply put, you cannot rely on a single marketing medium for generating leads. For strength and stability, a table requires all four legs. To lose one is to become less sound, less secure. So too with lead generation. Do you rely on a minimum of tactics, maybe to save a dollar? Or do you proceed with a strong and stable base? Lead generation is an iterative process; you must monitor and adjust your tactics based on your results.

For the complex sale, a proper lead generation program requires a disciplined and multimodal approach. A director of marketing comments: "I look at our lead generation efforts, specifically in this economy, as I might a financial portfolio. If I can't measure the tactics or programs in terms of return on

6 Figure 1.1 Cheryl Hatlevig, Chris Hawver, *Spheres of Influence*, 2005.

investment—leads generated, business closed, opportunities in the funnel—then why should I expect anyone to invest in my fund?"[7]

Valuable Tools to Use with Lead Generation

Let's briefly explore three key elements that are crucial for success with any lead generation program.

Closed-Loop Feedback Is Crucial

When routed to the sales department, many sales leads just disappear into a black hole, never to be seen again. Studies show that as many as 80 percent are ignored as a matter of course. This most probably is due to jaded salespeople accustomed to a tradition of poor-quality leads. With the proper universal lead definition, however, and with the sales team's input, there is justifiable confidence to believe that sales will ultimately close the loop and provide targeted results. How are we doing? Keep communication open. Relevant feedback is critical.

Database, CRM, SFA

For the purpose of clarity we will refer to the varied applications that track, house, and report on sales and marketing activity simply as a database rather

---

Discussion with the disgruntled vice president of marketing of one of the big software firms disclosed a poor success rate with lead generation companies he had worked with, and he was frustrated that his own internal lead generation program wasn't working either. Tangibly, things looked much brighter. The marketing department was decorated with beautifully framed, award-winning magazine ads. The CMO's office was like a toy store, with a wide array of logo-imprinted specialty items and a wall full of awards. None, suffice to say, was notated for ROI or its overall impact on performance. From a lead generation perspective, it would have been nice to see, for each:

- How many inquiries were generated.
- How many inquiries converted into qualified leads.
- How many sales were generated as result of that ad.
- What the ROI was.

---

7 Interview with Cheryl Hatlevig, Director of Marketing, Adesso Systems.

than customer relationship management (CRM) or sales force automation (SFA) with all the misconceptions and baggage that come with those terms.

Most companies still lack a defined process and discipline for consistently using and updating their databases. On average, salespeople are not held responsible for updating the databases, and marketers don't effectively know how to use the data contained in them. Unless the sales and marketing data are integrated, it is nearly impossible to get an accurate picture of return on marketing investment. Lead generation being the bridge between marketing and sales, the responsibility of maintaining the database must be assigned to one function or the other. Whichever, depending on the organization, it's important that the issue be addressed for the sake of managing the lead generation program.

Open Dialogue—A Mind-Set

As simplistic as it seems, *thinking effectively* is vital to developing good lead generation.

Our mind-sets ultimately influence our strategic choices. Investing in lead generation means you are proactively initiating a relationship. Lead generation becomes a conversation, a dialogue; it is not a series of campaigns. This opens up a whole new set of possibilities. Again, companies don't buy; people do. Good lead generation *identifies, initiates,* and *nurtures* relationships with the right people, making them sales-ready leads.

Chapter Two

Marketing and Sales: One Team in the Complex Sale

Collaboration Is Crucial

In chasing success with the complex sale, you might have the best mind-set, strategy, and tactics. You could have the finest team of sales and marketing people. But without the collaboration of everyone involved, you have little more than unrealized potential.

The collaboration of these functions can be likened to the batteries in a flashlight. If the batteries are not inserted in the right direction or are otherwise out of proper contact, their latent power is unusable. The interaction of sales and marketing is the same. If askew and going in dissimilar directions, sales and marketing will not empower a successful complex sale or sales lead strategy.

Inadequate or misdirected teamwork can be a plague to the complex sale. Common warning signs include performance-stealing personal frustration, lackluster sales effectiveness, and poor ROI. Bottom-line performance really reflects just how well the sales and marketing functions are working together.

The CMO Council, a noted invitation-only, high-level knowledge exchange for senior marketing officers, recently surveyed 800 senior marketing

Lead generation is everyone's business. If you are firmly committed to making it work, it is crucial that your entire organization be brought on board and understands its objectives. Without a show of hands at all levels, you can never achieve measurable success.

and C-level executives and found that just seven percent agreed that their sales and marketing departments were complementing partners in harvesting ROI from sales leads.[1] My own experience confirms that the communication breakdown between sales and marketing to one degree or another affects 9 out of 10 companies. Marketing customarily believes that salespeople, in their mad rush to close sales, are lone guns that ignore the recommendations extant in brand positioning. Sales, on the other hand, is convinced that marketing really doesn't understand how to help the sales team sell, and the information it provides is really of no help anyway.

The Aberdeen Group estimates that as much as 80 percent of marketing expenditures for lead generation and sales collateral is wasted because such outlays are regarded by salespeople as irrelevant and not very useful.[2] With the present-day intense pressure to demonstrate strong ROI, sales and marketing departments cannot afford to let the overhead expense of sales lead generation go to waste. The recurring disconnect between marketing and sales is a troubling challenge that must be dealt with head-on.

Not unlike military officers developing great strategy with frontline foot soldiers to execute their plan, there must be a spirit of conscientious follow-through in joint sales and marketing efforts with the expectation of winning. By virtue of doing a better job of integrating sales and marketing teams, companies not only enhance internal communication but also realize higher ROI from their lead generation programs. Such synergy helps organizations:

- Reduce sales and marketing expense.
- Increase ROI.
- Shorten sales cycles.
- Develop a more predictable sales revenue pipeline.

Question: Without a common sales and marketing goal, how can a marketing contribution to revenue be measured? Answer: Only with the necessary teamwork, assigned responsibilities, shared goals, and common objectives is that anywhere near possible. Even under such circumstances, measurement can be difficult and results fuzzy at best.

The lead generation program drives the sales pipeline. Most CEOs are frustrated with the seeming lack of activity at the beginning, or the top, of the sales funnel. The problem often is no more than insufficient follow-up by

1 "Gauging the Cost of What's Lost: Improve the Return on Resource Burn," (CMO Council, November 2004), p 11.

2 "Bridging the Divide: Process, Technology, and the Marketing/Sales Interface," *Market Viewpoint*, Vol 15 No 4 (Boston: Aberdeen Group, October 2004), p 1.

the sales department. As has been noted, the majority of sales leads end up on the cutting-room floor.

Assuming that one is familiar with the sales pipeline and has a good handle on measuring sales success, what are the buying process stages that must be defined and observed in filling it? Let's examine these stages more carefully, paying close attention to how teamwork can be developed at each stage.

Start with the Lead

Lead generation, consistently the most significant touch point between sales and marketing, is a key way to improve teamwork. To facilitate this, your company's sales road map must be in writing for all to see. Without a disciplined sales process within which everyone operates, a prospective customer's buying process is not readily identifiable, much less accurately tracked.

Actually, a single source within the selling company should have the responsibility to oversee the tracking, qualifying, and managing of leads until they are sales ready. Sending leads of whatever quality level directly to a salesperson is not good use of anyone's time—and certainly not the salesperson's time. What is really needed is an independent functionary to qualify all opportunities before they are handed over to sales. This process is called *lead qualification*. Once the lead is qualified, this middle person or team can even continue to have meaningful dialogue with the prospect via lead nurturing in the interest of identifying and capturing longer-term opportunities.

It is not accurate to say that generating more sales leads is the key to hitting revenue targets. As a matter of fact, most companies need to do a better job of managing the leads they already have. Effective lead management is significant to building a fluid sales pipeline. There is little point in adding more leads to a bad process precipitated by poor lead management when the result only consumes budgets and fosters wasted opportunities.

Alas, marketing and sales workflow is linear and seems bound and determined to go only in one direction. Without bidirectional communication, effective lead generation suffers greatly because there is no closed-loop feedback process. With a feedback process in place, however, each department will have a better sense of what the other department needs in order to accomplish its goals. In today's commoditized business environment, melding inherently diverse viewpoints and inputs is particularly important to a well-oiled marketing and sales machine that produces good sales leads and positive results.

Sales blames marketing for bad leads; marketing blames sales for poor follow-up. That is the nature of the beast. A corporate vice president of

..cently expressed this quite well when describing that in his ..perience there are two types of leads salespeople like to say they get from marketing: the new junk and the junk they already know about. The cheerless result? GIGO—garbage in, garbage out.

Fortunately, there is a solution for building two-way communication between marketing and sales, with the objective of seeing lead generation programs truly flourish and begin to generate real ROI. This solution should start with the top leadership in order to be successful.

The CEO's Role

A hard-charging CEO recently ranted, "I will not spend another dollar on marketing until our sales improve." Well, that might be a little extreme, but marketing cultures are predominantly top-down influenced by the wants and needs of the front office. The CEO, after all, shapes the vision of the company and sets the tone for its corporate culture and subcultures. If the individual at the top isn't an active supporter of marketing in the company, the proper environment for good, sound lead generation is far removed from reality. In many companies, as a result, lead generation becomes a bottom-up exercise that struggles to go anywhere.

The lack of synergy between sales and marketing is so common as to risk cliché. In many organizations, particularly those with focus in the business-to-business arena, the sales team rules. Oppositely, in business-to-consumer companies, marketing generally has the upper hand. Senior management wields strong clout in either case.

Like the complex sale, lead generation, with its many facets and interactions, can be properly sparked only by the CEO who believes in it. CEOs, in their position, probably feel the brunt of misaligned sales and marketing functions on an ongoing basis. By all indications, that is changing, with a pronounced swing in CEO ranks towards the pivotal role of marketing. More and more CEOs are focusing on interdepartmental collaboration and the attainment of the new strategic imperative, ROI measurement. Nonetheless, bad experience and unfortunate precedents can create resistance to change, and the CEO mind-set towards sales and marketing, bracketing lead generation, is still a knotty issue.

Changing the Culture

Lead generation focuses on the most crucial and strategic aspects of the company by developing new business relationships. Lead generation stalwarts are in the unique position of being catalysts for change. Ultimately, it becomes the job of the marketer to lead the charge in pursuit of success of the company's lead generation program. There remains no question, however, that a lot of others need to be part of the effort as well. By virtue of the all-inclusive, holistic approach to the complex sale, everyone must adopt the single objective of growing customer relationships. They can do this by thoroughly understanding the customer's needs. We'll explore this further in Chapters 3 and 5.

Setting strategy in place is easier than following through and executing its tenets. To communicate effectively and on the same wavelength, marketing and sales must develop a shared culture and speak the same language. Intranet portals, blogs, and extranets are possible ways to facilitate this and make it easier to collect and share competitive information. Salespeople can go to these sources to access templates, case studies, and articles that help move the sale along. In addition to all these resources, the best strategy is to have an open dialogue to obtain sales lead feedback such as:

- Was this helpful? Why? Why not?
- What else should we be doing?
- What other questions could we have asked to make the lead even better?
- What are we doing that we should stop?

Actually, in developing a lead generation program, it is incumbent on marketers to view the sales team as the customer. This is no different than directing a consulting firm project where the client is kept involved in each stage of the job. The sales team is thus so integrated that it has program ownership just like everyone else.

Talk is only one step, though. Sales and marketing may seem to be working together, but collaboration is more than just conversation. The concept of a holistic approach, where everyone has something to gain or lose from success or failure, first of all demands a shared vision. The restrictive, narrow view present in their own respective functions requires, instead, adoption of a much wider perspective that of the big picture. Vision, trust, and synergy towards the common goal, therefore, become proactively broad-based at every turn, in every action.

Once more, marketers must remember that their role is to help salespeople sell. Too often, the response is, "I have less budget but I'm expected to produce more. I'm faced with staff reductions. I have to measure our results, but I have no accountability with my colleagues and sales team." Marketers repeatedly ask how the marketing people can create any kind of successful lead generation program when the business culture invariably punishes them for everybody's lack of success. Nevertheless, if they don't help their sales department by providing qualified leads, they ultimately hurt themselves.

Other issues involved can make it difficult for marketing to provide sales with the best possible leads. One is the constant pressure to generate more sales *now,* which ultimately distracts marketers from the goal of generating only qualified leads. To alleviate comparable anxieties, salespeople fall back on the philosophy that it is easier to deal with the people you already know than to develop new relationships. This can result in leads that are not immediately sales-ready being forever ignored. Focusing on the opportunities and people you have dealt with before seems a natural response for sales. Unfortunately, it has a way of diverting the sales team from the best opportunities.

Another issue is associated with salespeople's propensity to believe that they own the customer relationship. While this may be accurate to the extent that much of the customer's perception of the company is based on personal interaction with the salesperson, it ignores the broader aspects of the concept of relationship building and the marketing role in it.

Yet another issue revolves around production of collateral materials for which marketing is responsible in the end. A study by the Aberdeen Group concluded that 40 to 60 hours of the salesperson's month is spent re-creating sales-ready, customer-relevant collateral material that the salesperson believed, sometimes with good reason, that marketing should have generated better in the first place.[3] Again, if there were more open communication and collaboration between the departments, this waste of valuable sales time wouldn't happen. Sales and marketing can preclude this by aiding in the collection and application of relevant and useful information that will expunge just about any duplication of effort, freeing up the time to acquire more customer relationships and grow the business together.

It is the marketing department's responsibility to develop a central library of collateral selling aids, available, ideally, in PowerPoint slide presentation form. These aids should ideally be customizable. Customizing might include a selection of value proposition statements, case studies showing how other companies have benefited from your solution, reference lists, product/service overviews, and anything else having to do with the specific selling situation. Other ideas that are quite effective and cost relatively little include invitations to participate in scheduled events or webinars that are

---

3 *Sales Effectiveness: Helping Sales Sell,* (Boston: Aberdeen Group, June 2004), p ii.

appropriate to their clients. Messaging, tailored to enhance the sales team's e-mail efforts, should be targeted, ongoing, and frequent.

Ultimately, with collaborative, proactive planning and execution, a lead generation program can be of immeasurable help in leveling the playing field by allowing you to succeed over your competition. All it takes is effort and commitment on behalf of both marketing and sales.

Sales and Marketing as Customers

It is just as helpful if sales thinks of marketing as its customer. If sales is "the other customer" to marketing, it stands to reason that marketing could just as well be a customer of sales. What is the upshot of marketing and sales regarding each other as customers? As designer and developer of the lead generation program, marketing automatically regards the sales force as its customer. It has made it its job to understand how salespeople work, what they value, the tools they need, and whether they can be sold on what marketing is doing. Sales, equivocally, wants to know its marketing "customer" for many of the same reasons in order to deal with it productively. Familiarity with its systematic processes is particularly important.

Customers—sales, marketing, or the real thing—have every right to express their satisfaction or dissatisfaction. The input garnered from compliments or complaints can be invaluable. Look on these remarks as important—and free—advice and direction emanating directly from the most important link in the chain.

Companies sensing the need for cooperation and teamwork sometimes believe they can perform miracles by reorganizing the sales and marketing departments. Interdepartmental reorganization appears to have little bearing on lead generation results. What matters most is having everyone on the same page, integrated, and viewing one another as pro forma customers.

Listen to your customers via your sales force before you try to meet their needs," says a recognized CEO and lead generation proponent. "Remember that the sales force is your customer. What do they consider a qualified lead and where are qualified leads found?

Share your ideas along the way and encourage feedback. Even issue the invitation to co-create a solution with you."[4]

---

4 Interview with Pam Van Orden, President, White Canvas.

Reorganization seems to work only when, historically, no one has been talking to each other and there appears little likelihood that they will.

Collaboration Is Key

A recent report by Aberdeen Group concludes: "The number one issue for most CEOs and marketers is lead generation—getting more leads to their sales team. The number one desire for salespeople, however, is MORE selling time with sales-ready opportunities."[5]

You must realize that the extreme time pressure salespeople face—especially those with a complex sale—requires them to ignore what is not immediately relevant and highly likely to produce revenue.

Given that it remains an issue, however, what can be done to facilitate a lead generation program without jeopardizing selling time? Begin by listening and communicating, by collaborating on the solution. Ask this question: "How can we give our salespeople more selling time?" Then write down your thoughts and meet with your sales team and ask them the same question: "How can we help YOU get more selling time?" Now be quiet and really listen.

Ultimately, the goal is to provide a continuing supply of high-quality leads that will pave the way to relationships of equal quality, which in turn will result in either bigger payoffs or follow-up and backup plans to prevent those hard-won leads from falling through the cracks.

The complex sale creates new sales lead rules for both marketing and selling. Typically, the rules should be as follows:

- Centralize the lead qualification process.
- Encourage salespeople to follow up on leads for which they will be held accountable.
- Encourage feedback from the sales team and carefully examine the conversion process with regular face-to-face meetings or conference calls.
- Understand where the sales team is and nurture it; do not force-feed leads at a time when their focus might be on closing important sales efforts.
- Develop a strategic lead generation plan, standardizing and documenting the sales process for purposes of tracking and measuring.
- Conduct frequent, regular meetings to stay tuned with developments.
- Share best-practice lead generation information.
- Assign revenue goals to joint sales and marketing plans.

---

5 "Sales Effectiveness: It's About Collaboration," *Perspective*, (Boston: Aberdeen Group, August 2004).

- Document the lead hand-off process and accountabilities at each stage.
- Be flexible.
- Promote lead generation from the top down and the bottom up.
- Develop a culture that values universal lead definition.
- Get the marketing team out into the field with the sales team regularly.
- Arrange compensation to reflect shared accountability vis-à-vis lead generation.
- Close the loop on each sales lead generated.
- Keep nonselling tasks the responsibility of marketing.
- Integrate sales and marketing into the same database.
- Define and map responsibilities shared by sales and marketing.
- Share PR opportunities.
- Continually reinforce lead generation program strategies.
- Share new insights gained from customer feedback.
- Jointly develop a message map and value proposition.
- Examine and apply what has been learned.
- Implement parameters from successful campaigns.
- React to and develop solutions for the prospect's concerns.
- Conform messaging to target audiences.
- Analyze and use competitive strategies as warranted.
- Improve sales tools and marketing materials.
- Map out the prospect's buying process.
- Determine the life cycle of a lead.
- Define your expertise in solving business problems and sharing solutions.
- Examine existing programs as possible strategic basis.
- Develop a strategy for lead nurturing.

Some of the challenges to generating sufficient high-quality leads include finding and focusing on prospects with the greatest likelihood of becoming profitable customers. Subsequently, through thorough evaluation, the sales-ready leads can be matched with the right sales individuals at the right time.

Customers, existing or prospective, expect that you know what your last conversation with them was about. They fully expect that the person calling them will have a totally retentive memory and all the answers. In the complex sale, so many people are involved in the process that it is imperative that pertinent information be captured in one centralized database. If sales and marketing are accessing and relying on different information databases, the snags tend to be insurmountable. Together, they can be amazingly effective. I'll explore the topic of the lead generation databases further in Chapter 4.

Marketing can render a lot of help to sales in the cultivation of opportunities. Perhaps the prospect fits the ideal customer profile but is simply not ready to buy yet. Marketing and sales can be an awesome force in working together to nurture such opportunities towards the time the prospect is considered sales ready. Marketing, taking the prospect's viewpoint, must think strategy rather than tactics. Strategy is the broad view, from multiple perspectives, with marketing on the point in developing joint programs with sales.

Focus on Collaboration

Ultimately, if you want to meet the goal of generating more revenue with less expense, marketing and sales must stand forth as an integrated entity. On a closed-loop basis and with two-way communication, it is amazing what can happen. In the complex sale, if you begin by focusing on so-called hot leads where the potential customer is already involved in the evaluation stage, you are too late. The early acquisition of research information on competitors, the marketplace, competition, and the target audience is crucial.

So, in perpetuating the effective partnership with sales, marketing's core efforts must center on:

- Measuring the contribution of marketing.
- Scoring leads and demonstrating their effectiveness on an apples-to-apples basis.
- Identifying and rectifying poor-performing strategies and tactics.
- Salvaging and reconstituting leads that were considered wasted.

And sales must focus on:

- Utilizing more sales-ready leads.
- Managing potential sales-ready leads better.
- Providing timely feedback to marketing.

The good lead generation program carries on a dialogue that is in concert with what the salesperson is saying. It is essentially a conversation, an exchange of information. When the focus starts with the customer's world and works back from there, lead generation is suddenly easier to implement. As he or she is in one-on-one conversation, so too must the salesperson be proactive in initiating exchange within the program. Ultimately, effective and efficient collaboration between sales and marketing leadership is wonderful and where we all want to be, but don't overlook the crucial necessity of corporate alignment from the top down and the bottom up as well. An important part of this alignment is having a universal lead definition, which we'll explore next.

Chapter Three:

Defining Your Best Lead

"The job of marketing is to develop a lead generation system that matches the readiness of the buyer with the expectations of your sales person."
—John Coe,
The Fundamentals of Business-to-Business Sales & Marketing[1]

Arbitrarily forcing a lead generation program on the sales team without its buy-in is sure to court disaster. As discussed in the previous chapter, the strategic ingredient of the complex sale is teamwork, where sales and marketing work together towards the common goal from the outset. And with a common voice in communicating not only to potential customers but from one to the other. This teamwork allows marketing to generate the right leads and sales to engage the right steps to facilitate the buying process.

A major step towards building teamwork is working together to collaboratively define what a sales-ready lead actually is. And to start building that definition, it is necessary to first create a profile of your ideal customer.

Target Your Ideal Customer Profile

To test water purity, testing equipment must be calibrated to a standard, without which there could be no accurate test results. Similarly, the ideal customer profile will be the main focus of how you spend your energy, time, and budget to determine the most productive opportunities.

The goal of the ideal customer profile is to focus on companies with the greatest likelihood of becoming profitable customers. A brainstorming session with a cross-functional team is an effective method for fleshing out all possibilities.

---

1 John Coe, *The Fundamentals of Business-to-Business Sales & Marketing*, (McGraw-Hill: August, 2003).

Target what are considered to be the best potential companies and contacts. Then make lists of the best and the worst of your current customers. What do they have in common with your list of prospective customers?

- Rank your customers by most profitable, best revenue, easiest to do business with. In reverse order, rank by least profitable, worst revenue, hardest to do business with.
- Evaluate the characteristics of each company to determine why the top five companies are on each list.
- Identify the key attributes that your best customers and worst customers share. What characteristics link the best and what characteristics link the worst?
- Then add current revenue and profitability data and any other information you deem important and rank your list of possibilities.

You will likely find that those at or near the top are accurate reflections of your ideal customer profile. Take the top and bottom customers and prospects and build a more detailed profile. Populate the profile with the following information:

- Annual revenue.
- Standard Industrial Code (SIC) and North American Industry Classification (NAICS).
- Number of employees.
- Level of contact you are working with and in what functional area.
- Local, regional, or national.
- Business situation, i.e., is the company in growth or decline?
- Psychographics aspects, e.g., corporate values, culture, philosophy, leadership, and internal/external factors that may be having an overt effect on the company.

Determine the most important attributes to replicate. It should be readily apparent that there is marked difference between those on the best customer list and those on the worst. For example, does a best customer show the inclination to be well-managed with long-term growth while a worst customer exhibits continual reorganization and declining revenues?

You will likely have other attributes that are specific to your industry. From there you will need to narrow attributes to the best 5 to 10. This list will serve as your ideal customer profile.

Realistically, there are many times where an opportunity has other strategic appeal even though it may not fit your ideal customer profile. Then it becomes a measure of how far an opportunity diverges from ideal. A potential but marginally nonideal opportunity can always be preempted during the sales process if necessary.

If you are launching a new company, product, or service, then you won't likely have this data readily available. Develop a profile of what you believe to be the likely fits. Are there ancillary ways of finding that data? Can you learn from your competition or indirect competitors?

Clearly Articulate Your Target Market

Before embarking on the lead generation program and developing your database, it's vital that you clearly articulate your target market. A successful approach includes taking the time to segment the target market in accordance with the unique priorities of the ideal customer profile. This will help you understand just how large the universe of available opportunities might be. I'll cover this process in more depth later.

The ideal customer profile becomes the standard that is applied against the total target universe. An example might be a practice target, as illustrated by Figure 3-1, with the outer ring representing 5,000 companies, the next ring 2,500, the next 1,000, and the center or "sweet spot," 500. The sweet spot best represents the ideal customer profile. However, make sure the remaining 4,500 companies are still a part of your lead generation program.

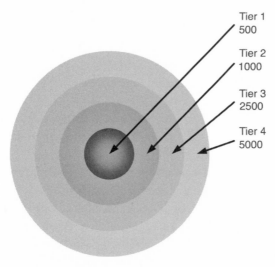

Figure 3-1 Target universe

Case Study

A client company wanted to increase its average sale, which had been about $60,000. It was advised to focus its resources on developing a database with prospects that fit its ideal customer profile, with lead generation efforts to reach the right people at these companies. In their first year of a new program, the average sale rose by more than 30 percent to $80,000, while overall revenue increased by 20 percent. As a result of developing the ideal customer profile, the sales team focused on fewer opportunities but of much higher quality. Contrary to initial fears, it became clear that effort required to make the larger sale paralleled that of the smaller sale. Profitability was also higher because reduced staff time required to service fewer tasks resulted in lower overhead expense.

The ideal customer profile is not an absolute; rather it helps bring focus to your broader base of prospects.

Do you know the size of your target universe?

The ideal customer profile helps you prescreen potential opportunities based on the unique attributes of your prime customers and serves as basis for the definition of a sales-ready lead. What do I mean by sales-ready lead? Let's examine that more carefully.

Inquiries Are Not Sales-Ready Leads

If you are in marketing, are you currently sending your sales team qualified leads or merely inquiries? There is a difference. An inquiry is an interested party who has requested information and needs some level of assistance. But inquiries are not leads.

Numerous lead qualification programs have shown that as little as 5 to 15 percent of all inquiries are truly sales-ready opportunities. Again, inquiries are not leads. If inquiries are sent to the sales team as "leads" without first being qualified against an agreed-upon definition, they are not sales ready and are more or less a waste of time for the sales team.

If sales leads are regularly of poor quality and don't yield results, it doesn't take the sales department long to conclude that they are all a waste of time. And without well-defined criteria of what constitutes a qualified sales lead, leads have little chance of improving or being accepted.

Quality over Quantity—It Matters

Few dispute the fact that a large quantity of leads, regardless of quality, does-n't guarantee that sales success will follow. Some consequences of quantity at the expense of quality are:

- **Sales team frustration.** Having an optimized lead generation program can become a key asset in recruiting and retaining great salespeople. However, if your sales lead generation program produces poor leads, it will negatively impact your seasoned sales reps as well as new sales-people.
- **Unfocused sales and marketing efforts.** Your salespeople spend their time pursing leads that are not sales ready yet. It is also likely they are ignoring others that they know little about. Ultimately, this will increase your average sales cycle.
- **Inaccurate sales forecasts.** If unqualified leads invariably make their way into the sales pipeline, business going forward will suffer.

The question that must be top of mind, therefore: Is this lead sales ready? This should be posed for every potential sales opportunity, as weighed against the lead definition criteria that sales and marketing have agreed upon.

What Is a Lead, Anyway?

So, what is a lead? At its most basic definition, a lead is a potential customer that wants to learn more about what you have to sell and that has acknowl-edged it has a business problem that you could help solve. Couple this defi-nition with elements from the ideal customer profile and you have the beginnings of a meaningful lead definition.

For the lead definition to be useful in its application, it must to be applied to all leads *regardless of source*, i.e., teleprospecting, Web site, inbound calls, direct mail, etc. The fact that the definition is applied to all sources is critical in implementing a lead management system, which will be explored later. And most importantly, it must be agreed upon by both sales and marketing.

A "qualified sales lead," then, by definition, is one that has been deter-mined to fit the profile of the ideal customer and has been qualified as sales ready according to the universal lead definition. The universal lead definition is that against which every potential customer is compared and prioritized as determined by where it is in its buying process and delineated by its degree of sales readiness, regardless of source.

What Makes One Lead Better than Another?

Salespeople often struggle with inconsistency in clear criteria. As a result, some opportunities are given too much focus while others are ignored.

In order to maximize the sales team's time, it is important that marketing knows how to differentiate an inquiry from a lead. This is also crucial to efficient use of the marketing budget; experience shows that leads qualified by the standard of a universal lead definition are pursued more diligently than leads that are not.

The universal lead definition acts as the standard for rating leads. A good universal lead definition needs to be basic and intuitive so that every sales and marketing participant is fully in tune with the definition. Even further to the point, everyone involved in the lead generation and selling process must agree and buy in to what a qualified lead really stands for.

Lead generation is a process that addresses consistency, vis-à-vis conformance with the ideal customer profile and universal lead definition. Applied consistency yields higher-qualified leads for maximum return on investment and ultimately more business.

The Hot Lead

Everyone has heard of the "hot lead" in one context or another, but have you ever wondered what that means? The hot lead reflects the degree of sales readiness, when from all indications that prospect is truly sales ready: by virtue of its conformance to the ideal customer profile and universal lead definition established for it, by the existence of a stated initiative and an obvious motivation to use your solution, by key decision makers being involved, by an identified short time-to-purchase time frame, by proactive evaluation activities and information exchange, and by a confirmed budget to facilitate a purchase.

A good lead by any description, "hot" or otherwise, benefits by application of the BANTS formula as illustrated by Figure 3-2:

- **Budget.** Does the prospect affordably mirror your ideal customer profile?
- **Authority.** Does it involve the important players in the purchasing decision process?
- **Need.** Has a clear initiative or need been acknowledged? Are they motivated?
- **Time frame.** Has it been determined when the purchase decision will take place?

Figure 3-2   Qualification criteria

- **Sales ready.** Is there comfort in the imminent prospect of meeting with a salesperson?

Caution—Hot Leads May Burn You

Leads most universally prized by salespeople, no matter the industry, are those with a decision time frame of less than three months. When it comes to the complex sale, these so-called hot leads may in fact be hard-to-win opportunities.

With a decision time frame that is quickly approaching, you may find that you are no more than column fodder—up against competitors that have been in discussions with the prospect for months and have already established themselves. You may be in an uphill battle with little time to gain a solid foothold.

For this reason, opportunities need to be identified as early in the prospect's buying process as possible. There must be a long-term lead generation and lead nurturing process in place to do that. And back to the point at hand: your definition of what a sales-ready lead is must take into consideration that sooner is not necessarily always better. A lead definition that helps identify the best possible opportunities rather than the fastest to close should be a major tenet when developing a universal lead definition.

Interestingly, research shows that top sales performers have the best opportunity-screening skills. They focus their energies where odds of winning are best, but more importantly they seem endowed with a sense of who will become ideal customers with more purchases, longer-term value, and greater profitability. Poor sales performers, conversely, focus on opportunities that have a high likelihood to close but may not necessarily yield the best customers. This may be why top sales performers succeed despite poorly executed lead generation programs.

If your lead generation program is off target, you stand to do more damage than good. When salespeople demand "hot leads," marketing can help them more effectively target their opportunities by jointly developing and applying the ideal customer profile and universal lead definition criteria.

Creating the Universal Lead Definition

Again, successful lead generation goes far beyond the marketing department and is a shared vision of many, underscored by the premise that all have everything to gain or to lose.

With supportive senior management enrolled, schedule a kickoff meeting where sales, marketing, IT, customer service, and other interested groups start to collaborate on the process of customer conversion.

- **Meet.** Get *all* those involved together and select a capable leader. Gather the sales and marketing teams in one room or via conference call. Add a facilitator who has street credibility and who speaks the language of both and get the air cleared. Everyone must be on board or this thing isn't going to make it.
- **Ask.** What do we consider a qualified lead? What are the characteristics of the ideal sales opportunity? What do we really need to know? What would be nice to know? Who should we be contacting? Who is involved in the buying process? What common needs are we addressing?
- **Meet again.** Is there consensus that we are on the same wavelength?
- **Expose.** Widely publish the universal lead definition in the interest of integrating it into the organization's culture and language.
- **Close the loop.** Marketing and sales should meet regularly to review and reconfirm the universal lead definition's efficacy—with such queries as: Was a particular lead an actual lead? Did it enter the sales process? Why or why not? What else should be known about it? How can we improve on what we are doing?
- **Edit and republish.** There is no reason the universal lead definition can't be improved on if required.

As you work together in your group to create your lead definition, you may find that certain persistent differences of opinion between departments and/or individuals are standing in the way of objective conclusions. Concerted effort has to be made immediately to correct this.

Criteria for the Universal Lead Definition

When working with clients, as previously suggested, we facilitate meetings and bring marketing and sales leaders together. A universal lead definition then begins to take shape in response to such interrogatories as:

- What makes a good sales lead?
  - What initiative or need makes this a good fit?
  - What information must you have to determine if a lead is worth the follow-through?
  - What are the titles/job functions of economic buyers/influencers?
  - What does this company value? What is its culture like?
  - What are the common business issues?
- What information do you want in order to qualify a lead as being sales ready?
  - How do you currently qualify a prospect? What questions do you ask?
  - What questions do you want answered before getting a lead?
  - What questions tend to gather the most needed information?
  - What information is must-have versus nice-to-have?
- How would you differentiate between near-term, mid-range, and long-range leads?
  - Will there be a time frame to evaluate and implement a solution?
  - Will there be a formal or informal budget in place? How much?
  - Are there specific behaviors or traits you are looking for?
- What functions or "buy points" are targeted in terms of key contact information?
  - How is interest created? Where does it start and what is it driven by?
  - What fuels interest and how do you focus on it with your solution?
  - What was the compelling event that drove their interest?
  - Who are the economic buyers and influencers involved in the decision?
  - Where is your best entry point?
  - Who usually needs to be contacted during the first phase of the sales process?
  - Who is involved as the buying process evolves?
  - Who or what tends to drive the initiative?

- Who else should be contacted?
- Where does the funding come from and who has authority over it?

Your answers should be collected and consolidated in a single document and routed to all stakeholders, ensuring that everyone is satisfied with the lead definition as written and no key points were missed.

A Lead Generation Fable

You are stranded in a desert. There is no civilization visible and worse, you have no food or water. After three days of walking you are cramping up, overcome by exhaustion and dehydration. The wind drives sand against your exposed face and neck. "One more sand dune," you say as you scale the next. Suddenly, your legs collapse and you roll down the other side.

You come to with vision blurred and try to wipe sand from your stinging eyes. As you turn your head, you notice the sun is setting, and in the distance, another mirage. You nearly give up hope. You have been days without water. Your mind is hazy; you try to focus. Nothing. As the sun drops, the shadows lengthen. Wait. Could that be a palm tree? You stagger towards the oasis. There's water! As you drink, finally, you know you have never tasted anything so wonderful. How much sweeter the water would have been without the presence of camel dung.

The moral? You can give salespeople, dying of thirst, even dirty water and they will drink it. But if they are not thirsty, they will not.

If they are satiated (busy closing a big deal) then you can almost bet that even clean water (sales-ready leads) will be ignored. If dehydrated, they will likely pursue any opportunities, even poor ones. And they will still want more.

To break this cycle, marketers must set the standard and strive to give salespeople—thirsty or not—only filtered water (sales-ready leads) that has been treated with reverse osmosis (universal lead definition and ideal customer profile). Only then will salespeople trust that every time they drink the water, it will be pure. Eventually salespeople will demand only the pure water, even if they are thirsty.

Making sure that a lead has a clear definition (that everyone has agreed to) and that it has been compared against your ideal customer profile is the best way to ensure that marketing does not deluge sales with too many leads at the expense of quality. Provide only the number of leads —good, sales-ready leads (pure water)—each salesperson can handle. By controlling the lead flow, the sales team has a better chance of actually developing relationships.

Case Study

A large utility company working with major energy users retained my company to develop and execute a lead generation strategy. The company was the result of multiple acquisitions. Services provided ranged from managing factory power stations to improving energy usage by large energy-consuming organizations like automotive manufacturers, government agencies, and state universities.

Despite lead generation programs implemented internally, there had been little traction among the divisions, and the sales pipeline was weak. The corporate CEO had spent considerable time developing shared culture and language among the acquisitions. The last areas to be integrated were the previously separate sales and marketing groups.

The corporate emphasis on collaboration and teamwork was significant to the philosophy that, as one, the multiple acquisitions would offer a better solution with cross-sell to larger customers as the goal. Results were disappointing, however. Senior sales management believed that this was because the three sales teams were using disparate sales methodologies and approaches to business development.

Collaboration and teamwork among the divisional sales teams was, in fact, virtually nil. Developing a universal lead definition, therefore, as a product of sales and marketing cooperation, was crucial to a mutual respect for and understanding of each unit's issues and ultimately the success of all.

In the end, we conducted an all-day universal lead definition workshop with divisional managers and front-line salespeople for purposes of creating a universal lead definition. It was important that we get consensus from everyone involved in attracting and getting customers, from the CEO to many line and staff functionaries.

By getting everyone together to jointly define the ideal customer profile and universal lead definition, they were able to collectively develop a common language that enabled more effective teamwork, more cross-selling opportunities between different groups, and greater return on marketing investment.

Each lead generation program this company uses now is better than the last, and results prove it. The sales team has become more productive, sales cycles are noticeably shortened, and new insights into the customer's needs are gained daily.

To effectively measure return on marketing investment and optimize sales effectiveness, you must centralize your lead management process. The first step is lead qualification, which we'll cover in the next section.

Using the Universal Lead Definition to Qualify Leads

Naturally enough, the ideal customer profile helps qualify potential customers up-front. With work on the universal lead definition completed, the next step is for the marketing team to qualify all leads by the process of lead qualification.

Lead qualification is a process that focuses on rating and scoring all inquiries, regardless of source, according to your universal lead definition. By using a lead qualification process, your sales team can rest assured that they will only receive truly sales-ready leads. By way of example and as illustrated in Figure 3-3,[2] SiriusDecisions has developed a lead level spectrum that is helpful in defining where a prospect or lead is in the buying process.[2] This sales lead spectrum can be used in support of the more detailed universal lead definition. The spectrum is an effective tool in deciding when a lead should be handed off to sales. With an agreement in place as to what level of leads sales should take, it ensures that these opportunities are handed off at the appropriate time. Interestingly, high-performing companies seek to send level-three leads or greater to their salespeople and they tend to have much higher ROI from their lead generation programs as a result. This confirms my premise that sending inquires over to your sales team before prospects are further along in their buying process is not effective. In Chapter 18, I will outline the process of lead nurturing, which will help you move your low level leads or inquires to higher level leads that you can confidently hand of to your sales team.

This lead qualification process must inspire the confidence of the sales team by being given only viable sales opportunities. Many organizations have created internal departments or hired third-party firms to assist in the task of qualifying leads from inquiries.

Once it is known where the leads fit into the sales process—and the customer's buying process—the appropriate marketing actions can be determined. This allows nurturing of leads that aren't yet sales ready, and, where necessary, the sales team can hand leads back to marketing for further qualification. In

2 Figure 3-3, "SiriusDecisions Demand Creation Facts & Figures 2005," (Southport, CT: SiriusDecisions 2005).

Level 1	A response from an individual to a marketing campaign or someone who has taken proactive steps to demonstrate interest in your message, product, or service.
Level 2	A meaningful interaction (via phone or e-mail) with an individual meeting the requirements of a fully qualified company and audience.
Level 3	Level 2 plus the individual demonstrates a specific need for and interest in your product or service.
Level 4	Level 3 plus the individual is in the process of defining a requirement for your product or service.
Level 5	Level 4 plus the individual has the responsibility, budget, and a defined timeline for the purchase.

Figure 3-3   The SiriusDecisions lead spectrum

lead scoring situations, leads that fall below a certain threshold can be held back. If some leads fall out of the sale pipeline altogether, they can be recycled and further nurtured.

Creating a lead qualification process that works is challenging, and many companies do not succeed at the outset. With open and honest communication, however, including a closed-loop feedback mechanism for the sales team to use easily, the process is eminently doable.

Lead scoring is the method of assigning a numerical value (points) to responses gathered during the lead qualification process. A lead, classified by the universal lead definition criteria, is weighted based on the sales process. Added up, the lead criteria points yield a final score that, when meeting a predetermined threshold, is the basis for transferring the lead to sales.

Lead scoring can be complex and often begins as a relatively uncomplicated grading system that is then gradually enhanced as the process gets up and running. Lead scoring is only recommended when there is a large number of inquiries to screen. The numerous variables to weigh in screening suggest that the process should be as uncomplicated as possible at the outset, before attempting a scoring system. Lead scoring does afford visibility into the lead pipeline as well as the sales pipeline.

It doesn't matter what name your company calls a lead as long as it is meaningful to the sales force. Call it anything you want, but be certain that it carries weight with the sales team. It need not be complicated. As a matter

I facilitated a universal lead definition meeting with a new client that had previously formulated an internal quick-and-dirty lead definition. The company sought to relaunch its lead generation program with stronger buy-in from the sales team.

The director of marketing had heard caustic comments from the sales team about the quality of leads her department had generated before. She brought the meeting to a quick halt, explaining that she would get together with each salesperson one-on-one to work out issues pertaining to the previous program, in the interest of starting with unanimous agreement on sales lead definition this time.

This ultimately added an extra three weeks to the launch of the program, but the resulting consensus on the proper lead definition ensured the sales department's total buy-in. With the same tactics and budget as the previous program, return on investment was 120 percent greater than before. The full agreement of sales and marketing on a universal lead definition was credited as being the crucial success factor.

of fact, keep it simple and it will evolve to your continuing benefit over time; crawl, walk, and then run.

Salespeople don't care if a lead is A, B, C, or Q. All they really care about is whether the leads they receive are sales ready. They will not adjust their behavior just because marketing classifies a lead as having a score of 200 instead of WARM. Most follow the path of least resistance to get to the destination of making quota. Communication, teamwork, and shared vision are, as a result, essential.

Lead generation is an iterative process and it needs to be continually refined. Refining requires real data and feedback. To that end, marketing and sales must meet regularly, by whatever means, e.g., teleconferencing, sales get-together, etc.

The distributed energy of sunlight doesn't have the same force as the concentrated energy of a laser beam, and a laserlike focus is the key to an ideal customer profile and universal lead definition.

Choose your prospective customers carefully, always with a view towards achieving:

- Higher-qualified, sales-ready leads.
- A sales force with less frustration.
- Increased sales effectiveness.

- More accurate sales funnel management.
- Shortened average sales cycle.
- Fast adjustments and early insight.
- Prioritized efforts for a good lead-nurturing program.
- Sales force accountability.
- Measured effectiveness of the lead generation investment.

The ideal customer profile and universal lead definition work together to help you focus on the customer, which makes for a better customer. What's the long-term value of that customer? The payoff is in proportion to the investment, which starts with a clear picture of the ideal customer and follows through the process.

Chapter Four

Lead Generation ROI Depends on Data Quality

Your Database Is a Valuable Asset

There is an old expression that says if you have eight hours to cut down a tree, spend six hours sharpening your ax. So it goes with creating the marketing database for companies that specialize in the complex sale.

The marketing database is crucial to any lead generation program. Experts agree that it can influence the program's success by a factor of 50 percent. Unfortunately, it still is one of the most overlooked tools in many companies' lead generation strategies.

The basic database likely will consist of such elements as revenue data, number of employees, geography, and related reference essentials. Far beyond that, many companies regard their database as a tangible way of measuring corporate goodwill, which can be treated as an asset on your financial balance sheet. Inadequacies in the database, conversely, can have a major negative impact with respect to all of the lead generation program's facets.

Maintaining a clean, updated database is unequivocally essential to the success of any lead generation program. Unfortunately, it is a necessity that is still flagrantly overlooked. Maintenance of the marketing database is an ongoing struggle for many organizations. Often it is tedious work. Whether there are 500 or 500,000 records, all have to be as up-to-date as possible. The never-ending vigilance for identifying and removing duplication and redundancies can be daunting. New businesses come, others go, others merge; all of the dynamics must be reflected in the database. And the difficulty of keeping sales and marketing teams accountable for their database maintenance responsibilities is double the trouble. The time and effort required, however, are paid back many times over.

The Database Is the Hub

A properly designed and maintained database is the well-oiled hub of all lead generation activity. It represents the rallying point for collaboration between marketing and sales. It can also foster cooperation among other groups in the organization, including those interfacing with customers, e.g., solution implementation, front-line customer service, accounts receivable, and such others as corporate management and research and development. While the focus here is primarily on the how effectively marketing and sales co-exist, the inherent need for teamwork among all contributors cannot be ignored.

Because many people are involved in the complex sale, it is important that the abundance of useful information about a prospect is captured in a single central location that can be accessed by everyone. The centralized database, for example, provides instant availability of record updates by lead to all other team members. Marketers can see and track the immediate results of their efforts, permitting ongoing adjustments, and it gives salespeople a reliable means of transmitting their feedback to marketing.

The Centralized Database

A centralized database is a system—or often a series of interrelated systems— that collects and consolidates information from various sources into a uniform format.

In some cases, this may be a customer relationship management system, known as a CRM. The CRM is software, methodologies, and related technologies employed in managing customer relationships. While the CRM can be the chosen vehicle for the centralized marketing database, it is by no means a required option.

The centralized database can integrate and share information across multiple database systems, but it does not have to be that one big utopian entity that has and does everything. For most organizations, the do-all/end-all capability represented by a system of that magnitude is simply not practical.

In the precomputer era, information was laboriously tracked manually and the paper records that were created were maintained in a manila file folder for each and every evolving sales lead. This folder full of information would make its way from one operative to another. A lead generator would update the information as required, and when it was ready would relay the folder to the salesperson to initiate the selling process. Afterward, assuming the sale was ultimately closed, the salesperson would pass the folder on to the implementation team. If the sale did not close, the folder might have gone back for further lead generation development. In all events, as the folder moved from person to person, task to task, everything relating to the lead went with it.

In principle, today's database—the centralized database—accomplishes the same thing but with information-age speed and thoroughness. From it flow the facts required by the various participating individuals or units. Control of the lead passes from one person to the next with all of the applicable information fixed in one place.

When pertinent data is available to everyone, the destructive impact of so-called information silos (where the focus is inward and all communication vertical) is eliminated. Far too many companies, however, still have sales and marketing operating in these information silos; managers serve as information gatekeepers, precluding timely coordination and communication among involved departments or functions, and the information needed for lead generation feedback is thus not available when most required. The natural tendency of management is then to assume that everything is okay. Meanwhile, salespeople are not getting the sales-ready leads they need to maintain their confidence that the process is working, with the result that there is unnecessary work, higher costs, poor results, and eroded relations between sales and marketing.

Under such circumstances, without centralization, the data tends to get lost in a myriad of campaign-driven lists, e.g., a teleprospecting list, a direct mail list, an e-mail list, ad infinitum. No one is on the same page. Each marketing entity maintains its own data, and information mayhem is the result. When information is required, the seeker has to go hunting for it, with increased effort and at added cost—if the information can be found at all.

The pitfalls are totally avoidable with the centralized database. An even more compelling benefit is the accelerated lead production that will result, not to mention customer retention and growth. As the lead passes through each station along the way, new opportunities seem to manifest themselves. A salesperson about to close a sale learns of a new potential opportunity that can instantly be brought to the attention of the lead generation team for qualification and follow-up. Or a teleprospector learns of a customer management situation that customer service should know about immediately.

The centralized database permits analysis of dead-end leads—those that have gone nowhere—and use of them as learning tools. There have to be reasons the opportunity was lost. Why did it not become a sale? Is the universal lead definition flawed? Perhaps the methods are misdirected? With a centralized database, the reasons can often be identified and applied towards making future activities more productive.

The dead-end lead itself may still harbor the potential to become a solid sales-ready opportunity. Significant time and effort were invested in collecting data on it, all of which remains banked in the database. Why not evaluate everything that originally made this a sales-ready lead and put in back into the machine for requalifying and nurturing?

When you develop the database, it's crucial to include a feedback mechanism should the process ever break down. Without this mechanism, the normal response for most companies is to create a "work around" solution to meet the immediate need. Quick-fix solutions may produce an immediate, short-term, positive result, but they may also wreck the very processes that are essential to the program's success.

In the end, the physical database itself cannot drive sales. A database is of little value to an organization without a commitment by all—in concert—to use it and use it properly. CRM can be quite right and proper for some companies but not for all. The promises of CRM to close more business and increase sales revenue are largely without substantiation in the broad view, and the hard fact is that CRM implementation is frequently synonymous with failure in those companies that blindly adopt CRM as the magic bullet. But don't blame the software as the reason for failure when such things as a breakdown in the sales and marketing collaboration could very well be the cause of lost sales. Good collaboration must exist before you implement any tool—such as CRM software. I've never seen collaboration suddenly develop as a result of it, especially between sales, marketing, and information technology.

Information Technology: Friend or Foe?

Clearly, the database is an amazing tool for both sales and marketing departments, and its success requires strong collaboration between these departments. It also requires collaboration with another department, information technology. Typically, the information technology (IT) staff creates and implements the database. For one reason or another, the IT team often doesn't see eye to eye with the sales and marketing teams, just as sales and marketing teams often don't see eye to eye with each other. Truth be known, most of this is due to basic misunderstanding—or lack of understanding—of each other's respective roles in the program, and right or wrong, IT specialists seem to have a history of not grasping the overall goal.

In some cases, marketers and salespeople are kept at full arm's length by their IT peers. Sadly, in spite of the business they are in, the sales and marketing teams of a database management firm we have worked with rely on an uncoordinated, haphazard system of spreadsheets for their company's database needs. IT people have not been enlisted as team members and consequently don't understand the value that they can bring!

No more, no less, the kind of collaborative relationship that is so necessary for sales and marketing must extend to and include the IT team if the development of the database is to proceed satisfactorily. And there is no rational reason for depriving IT people of a full slate of particulars when they are asked to become members of a joint effort. In spite of the esoteric and sometimes alien world of information technology, sales and marketing must take pains to "speak the language" and get comfortable with the fact that it is IT's responsibility to carefully and critically root out the problems in new initiatives.

Developing the Database

Building the database is not as complicated as might be imagined. If the ideal customer profile and the universal lead definition have been developed and brought up to speed, you are already a good share of the way there.

Acknowledging that teamwork is the crux of good lead generation practice, it should be obvious that the ideal customer profile and the universal lead definition are products of a collaborative endeavor—from which emanates the course of strong database design. The sales team has a place in the process, the marketing group has a place in the process, and the IT staff has a place in the process. This triumvirate is wholly responsible for making the centralized database what it is, the backbone of the program.

In practice, the database should indeed reflect attributes specific to the ideal customer profile and the universal lead definition. Corresponding fields are subsequently built into the database to properly prioritize and direct lead generation actions. Such fields may be tied to:

- Industry identification and description. The most common source of industry reference information is the Standard Industry Classification (SIC) code. SIC codes are four-digit numbers assigned to a wide array of industries by the U.S. Department of Labor.
- Annual revenue. An accepted means of gauging the size of companies.

Unique Identification Number

Every lead entry in the database is given its own unique identification number. This number facilitates tracking each opportunity as a separate record and prevents confusion among a vast assortment of leads and variables. Why not simply index by company name? Company names have been found to be notoriously imprecise for identifying specific leads, first, obviously because there are too many companies with the same or similar names. A recent search by company name yielded 42 matches. Secondly, where multiple opportunities exist within a single organization, there must be a way to go to the one you want.

- Employee size. Another way to gauge the size of companies.
- Geographic information. Metropolitan area, state, region, country, are required for targeting specific regional markets.
- Budget. Important if the universal lead definition specifies budget limits.
- Decision time frame. For chronological tracking when a deadline is indicated.

Regardless of the variables, all databases will almost always include these fields:

- Company name.
- Address.
- Telephone and fax numbers.
- Contact names and titles.
- Web site URL.
- E-mail addresses.
- Division/subsidiary/parent company relationship.
- Unique identification number.

Figure 4-1 illustrates a generic blueprint for a lead generation database layout. In practice an actual database will likely track more fields than are shown in this figure.

Other Important Fields

Marketers wonder what happens in the black box when they hand off a lead to the sales team. Because they use the same system and a shared process, both marketing and sales have access to information that can readily lead to

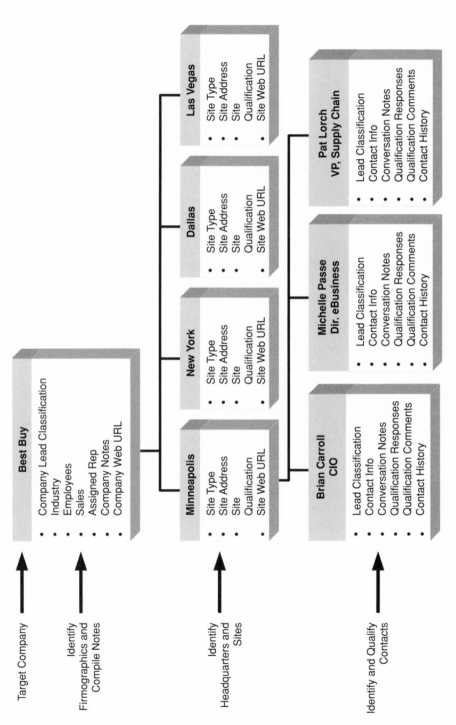

Figure 4-1 Lead generation database layout

47

closing the loop in assuring and measuring sales team performance. Tracking or status fields can help track leads through the entire process. These fields can include:

- Status codes. Where the lead is in the process.
- Assignments. Leads assigned to a specified salesperson and/or lead generator.
- Activity dates. The lead's most recent activity or next anticipated activity.
- Lead source. The lead's origin (essential for tracking return on individual marketing efforts).
- Forecasting tools. Close probability and estimated revenue for sales planning.

These fields enable tracking progress in the sales pipeline where a status code mechanism reflects the various steps in the sales process. A sales process would logically include these steps:

- New record.
- Teleprospecting.
- Sales-ready lead.
- Needs analysis.
- Proposal.
- Contract negotiation.
- Signed contract.

Each lead can be tracked and segregated by the status code field. Additional intermediate steps could be tracked, but steps defined should be identical to the lead generation and sales processes. With this tracking, specific points of failure or success are identifiable. For example, you may find that despite generating plenty of sales-ready leads, none is going to the proposal stage very often. This could mean that the lead definition is not specific enough, or perhaps that there are problems in the proposal process. By carefully tracking leads, you give yourself a great opportunity to improve the overall process.

Database changes must keep pace with the status of your company and its operations. It is too easy to get locked into a database format that takes an act of Congress to adjust. Not to belabor the obvious, but everything is subject to change: state of the business, value proposition, ideal customer profile, universal lead definition. The database must be flexible to reflect these changes as they occur, with IT team and policy that can make it happen.

Database Normalization

Database normalization is a way of efficiently organizing information in the database. From an IT perspective, normalization ensures speed and storage efficiency. For the marketer, it provides for easier maintenance of accurate data.

The most common normalization tactic uses select list fields as opposed to free text fields. The difference can be illustrated by imagining how to identify which of three salespeople is responsible for a particular record. Without normalization, an open text field would require typing in the name of the person, which leaves you at risk of error, typos, or unacceptable name forms. A select list field eliminates the chance of misstating information in that it requires that the name be chosen from a predetermined list of names that are ready and waiting in the database.

Normalized fields are used whenever there is a finite, distinct list of possibilities to be entered. These offer the most clear, concise reporting options that essentially categorize data into distinct buckets of data offered for analysis. On those occasions when free text information is required, the following are best practices that can be observed to keep data entered as clean and easy to retrieve as possible:

- Use proper capitalization, punctuation, and standard abbreviations, especially in address and name fields.
- Standardize a form for telephone numbers, etc.
- Uniformly structure addresses, e-mail, etc.
- Enforce minimum and maximum values for numeric and date fields.

As you move the database through its development, evaluate the field lists individually and determine what you expect of each, always with the thought in mind that the information must be to a standard that ensures accessibility in the future.

Reports

Reports are the window to the database and the means by which vital feedback can be brought to bear on the program's progress. An underdeveloped reporting system is usually the downfall of database systems, especially those with CRM implementation. It is important to address reporting requirements early in the database design process in light of their marked effect on desired fields. As many and varied as they may be, all reports have one thing in common: they respond to an intrinsic question. Some sample questions are:

- How many leads are we passing to sales each month or quarter?
- What has happened with each of our inbound Web leads?
- Who is the top-performing teleprospector?
- What is the return on investment for direct mail-generated leads?
- How many leads fit the ideal customer profile?
- Where are the major points of deviation from the ideal customer profile?

Some questions are exceptionally specific; you may be seeking a number or a single statistic. Others are instead a detailed record-by-record analysis of the database as a whole. In framing the questions, do it with a sense of how you expect the answers to configure.

Adding Data to the Database

Collecting data to populate the newly designed database is next. Keep in mind that there is no such thing as the perfect list from which to draw the information you seek. The best list is one that you create yourself from a variety of sources and that provides you the latitude to manage it against program objectives. Existing internal or in-house lists are the place to start, from such sources as:

- The sales team.
- Inbound phone, e-mail, and Web inquiries.
- Trade show attendees.
- Past marketing campaigns that generated names.
- Past customers.

A client was chagrined to be losing two percent of its clients each month during their contract renewal cycle. Procedurally, as a matter of course, the sales team would sell a three-year contract and move on, usually without inputting to or otherwise updating the corporate database. A program was developed to call the top 1,000 customers on the database, accounting for a good share of the company's revenue. It was found, however, that 65 percent of the original contacts were no longer with the customer or had moved to another position within the company. By carefully updating the database, the client stemmed its losses and, along with resolving attendant customer service issues, quickly began adding new business by generating leads with existing customers.

Mastering Verification

Updating a database is a daunting challenge for many. The verification process is like trying to hit a moving target. It has been shown that better than 70 percent of businesspeople change one or more elements on their business cards each year, and companies are continually in a state of flux with name and title changes, mergers, acquisitions, bankruptcies, and divestitures. As a result, obviously, continuity of the database can fall out of line in the proverbial heartbeat. It is therefore important to recognize that verification is forever an ongoing process. Though probably never 100 percent accurate, the rate can be kept within acceptable limits with assiduously alert attention for changes and promptness of revisions to the database on the part of all concerned.

Once these lists are picked and are in hand, they are normalized to fit the database design. They must also be collated and checked for duplication, known as "deduping."

As the in-house lists are consolidated, they should be customarily evaluated for compliance with the ideal customer profile before going on to database record status. You will probably find that the information they contain frequently has to be augmented to one degree or another as well.

There are many and varied outside sources of lists of every imaginable description, and though external lists have their individual benefits and drawbacks, they must be carefully evaluated on the strength of their maximum potential value to the specific lead generation program under development and on the basis of:

- Whether the list is for sale or for rent. Rented lists restrict use, application, and time and are generally not appropriate to ongoing lead generation programs.
- The actual data content contained. For lead generation, basic demographic data and phone numbers or other means of contact are important.

The best lists come from data companies like Dun & Bradstreet and InfoUSA because they include the demographic data typically needed as well as extended contact information. Their drawback, however, is that they are somewhat limited general business directories, and a wider net often needs to be cast in the hunt for data that fits the ideal customer profile.

Using the Database

Most people are surprised when putting the completed database to work is more difficult than designing the database. For the database to serve fully and successfully, the commitment to teamwork established early-on must be observed and complied with in the regular application of the database function. Get the salespeople on board early and continue to encourage their consistent and disciplined use, predicated on:

- They were an integral part of its development from the beginning.
- They have been convinced that it will improve their results.
- They are comfortable with its ease of use.
- There are available channels for their continued input and support.

In the final analysis, the sales folks must know that the database is a vital component of the program requiring their collaborative commitment to keeping it dynamic and functioning. Marketing should respond immediately to their feedback and work in all practical ways to maintain their awareness.

Regular and consistent updates as records flow through the system help maintain the accuracy and relevancy of the data, requiring, again, the commitment of everyone taking part in the lead generation program.

The practice of lead nurturing, which connects closely with frequent, meaningful contact with leads and potential sales leads, can reveal all manner of valuable new or updated information. Lead nurturing is, day-in and day-out, the best source of updated data.

You may choose to employ someone for regular and ongoing telephoning to the database for data verification. Other points of contact, e-mail and direct mail, for instance, can serve a similar purpose. E-mail that is bounced back and direct mail that is returned are often indications that contact information has changed. Still, to update the new information may require the phone call.

The task of adding data and appending with new information from other sources seldom stops. All of the additions require filtering, cleaning, normalizing, and deduping before going on record. Appending, incidentally, differs from adding new records in that it is purely an updating procedure for records that already exist.

Without question, the database, properly designed and used, will improve your lead generation efforts tremendously. Its value, however, is only as good as the buy-in of everyone who subscribes to it as a necessary part of day-to-day lead generation activities, aided and abetted by a sales team that feels the database helps do the job better and an IT team that knows exactly what is expected of it.

Chapter Five

The Value Proposition

Do you offer your potential customers all the reasons they should buy your solution? Do you enlighten them with your company's attributes? Do you tell them about your great people, your proprietary process, and your superior technology? Your product-to-market and operational excellence? All of your assertions are probably as good as can be, but chances are your competitors are saying the same about themselves. To which your prospect responds, "So what?"

The "old way" of selling arguably doesn't work anymore. Branding, awareness, and market share are still relevant to the complex sale, but a shift has taken place. Information that once required major effort to get, and often at not insignificant cost, is now easily accessible and free of charge, e.g., articles, annual reports, reviews, blogs, newsletters, portals, analyst viewpoints, the media, and numerous other trusted sources. The emerging onrush of the Internet is the big reason for this shift. No longer can we control a single message going out to our target audience. Potential customers are inundated with information and contradictory marketing messages from the competition. Because they are being influenced by numerous messages, they see that there are even more ways to address a single business issue—but are not always sure which business issue they need to fix. At times it is easier and safer for them to do nothing rather than risking the wrong choice.

For this very reason, it is wise to preemptively contact and develop relationships with our ideal customers. Quite literally, when we begin a conversation with them, their attitudes and beliefs are being shaped, primed by the information they have already soaked up through these various sources.

Regardless of the industry, 10 percent of potential customers are actively in search of a solution and have an inclination to buy what you sell. Another 10 percent may be interested in knowing about your solution but are "just looking at the moment." Thus, the reality is, 80 percent of your target market has no particular knowledge of or interest in what you have to offer. If you are launching a new product or service, this will be even higher.

The decision-making process has changed. The new laws—the Sarbanes-Oxley Act, for example—have promoted increased scrutiny, slower growth, and sharper margins, and the buying process for the complex sale has become elevated to senior executive levels. The lead generation program now needs to reach into the highest levels of a company; many involved in the buying process before are today influencers at best and certainly not the economic buyers they once were. Interestingly, many lead generation campaigns don't seem to get this. Rather, they continue to relegate top executives to a secondary position in the buying process and as a result totally miss the ultimate decision makers.

And the option if the potential market doesn't regard you as priority at the present time? Develop a strategy to commence conversation with the right people. You want to be the first resource they go to when the need for a solution arises, of course, so a sales team of trusted advisors becomes a great facilitator of that. Trusted advisors have established the confidence that they know what is relevant. This relevance is a personal thing. It represents a genuine understanding of the customer's business situation, needs, and desires and is perceived as exactly that throughout the lead generation program.

The path taken here thus far, therefore, hinges on how important it is to employ an ideal customer profile, a mapped-out universal lead definition, a legitimate database, and alignment with the sales team's selling process. From this comes conversation that begins to infuse your understanding of the prospect's world, concerns, and business needs, with a successful lead generation program the result.

What about Brand?

People often buy on emotion and backfill with logic. That's why *brand* is such a focus of time and marketing dollars in the business-to-consumer sector. It's more about perception and emotion than any real logic. Does it feel good? Brand is more often about a general idea that can appeal to many different customers at the same time. There is usually little or no education that needs to take place as the product or service's purpose or value is self-evident. The more awareness you generate, the more sales will likely result. And there typically is a much shorter time frame from message to purchase decision. For the most part, this is okay because the potential risk for a poor purchase decision by an individual consumer is often fairly low.

In the business-to-business market, however, there is much more at stake, particularly in the complex sale. A poor purchase decision can negatively affect an entire organization and have financial and operational ramifications that might persist for years. So it's not surprising that buying decisions in the area of the complex sale or business-to-business tend to involve multiple decision makers, a great deal of education, and much longer sales cycles. Organizations simply cannot afford to make purchase decisions based on a perception created through branding, no matter how compelling that impression may be.

In light of the challenges posed in the complex sale, marketers cannot afford to focus their budgets on building brand through traditional advertising when broad-scale media are so costly and lack the proper targeting. In short, a good reputation leads others to make conclusions about the corporate brand, but the corporate brand itself does not create reputation.

Reputation is rooted in value proposition and aligns with such notions as:

- Brand awareness is not enough. How you support salespeople in building relationships as trusted advisors, in turn builds reputation. Potential customers know, "How you sell me indicates how you will serve me."
- Tactics like thought leadership, public relations, and analyst coverage are more effective than traditional advertising efforts. These build trust on the strength of outcomes and capabilities.
- It is important to understand your potential customers' buying process. Your message must be in keeping with the needs of decision makers and influencers throughout the buying process.

A strong reputation is essential in the complex sale. The goal of lead generation is to connect your value proposition with the target audience's need. To attain that, salespeople are obligated to maintain contact with those customers or prospects that have a clear initiative, want to do something about it, and can satisfy your lead definition criteria as being sales ready.

Clearly articulating a value proposition is a crucial first step in connecting your brand, your reputation, and your potential customers' unique needs.

The Value Proposition Matters

Jill Konrath, author of *Selling to Big Companies* and recognized for her ability to formulate strong value propositions, says: "If it is a constant struggle to get into big companies and executive buying levels, you probably have a weak

I interviewed a partner in a 200-person e-commerce firm that was struggling with growing beyond the company's core client base. New business development results from lead generation were reported as "abysmal." When asked what had to happen to make that better, the individual responded, "We need to be meeting with more senior executives." I asked what was being done that would be considered relevant to the senior executives being targeted. She said that the company provided a self-service Web transaction platform to take orders online. After visiting a competitor's Web site, I suggested that she compare it with her own firm's Web site side-by-side. There was little or no difference in how they were positioned. It was therefore obvious that attention needed to be devoted to creating and sustaining a perceived difference that portrayed her company as having more to offer.

value proposition. Pure and simple. Wishy-washy and unfounded statements about the benefits customers get from working with your organization are likely the root cause of your lead generation problems. Without a supporting strong value proposition, it's hard to sell in today's economy, much less get your foot in the door."

For prospective customers, a value proposition essentially answers the questions of how can you help my business, what difference can you make, and why is your solution the one I should buy?

Jill Konrath further resolves: "A value proposition is a clear statement of the tangible results a customer gets from using your products or services. It's outcome focused and stresses the business value of what you have to offer."[1]

A strong value proposition opens doors and creates opportunities for the sale. It lines up with the financial side of things and speaks to the crucial issues of the target market. Specific, often right down to numbers or percentages, it may capsulize your work with similar customers and demonstrate just how compatible you can be.

A value proposition isn't a case of creating ideas in a vacuum, filling in blanks on a template, nor is it to a simple formula. If it were that easy, everyone would have one and the complex sale would likely be less than complex. Rather, it goes together in a process that depends on how you want the specific potential customer to perceive you as a contributing partner.

At the outset of the lead generation process, it is often a good idea to start with a value proposition that would be hypothetically appealing to the

1 Konrath, Jill, *Selling to Big Companies*, Dearborn Trade Publishing, 2005.

defined ideal customer. The value proposition then becomes specific to each lead contact as it moves through your company's sales process.

Developing Your Value Proposition

Communication and messaging always go right to the potential customer's needs, not to your own. Once more, the objective is to provide useful and relevant information that will reinforce the notion that this firm should buy from you. As the value proposition takes shape, it should be at the top of your mind that:

- It focuses on the contacts within your ideal customer profile.
- The potential customer has business issues that it needs—and wants —resolved.
- The potential customer must know the difference between opting for your solution and doing nothing.
- The potential customer must be convinced that you represent the best solution.

Before you begin, qualitative and quantitative research of your customers and prospects is necessary to validate your assumptions. Qualitative research enables an in-depth understanding of relevancies. It may be one-to-one communication, face-to-face, or by phone, but generally always centers on individuals or small groups. The technique is essentially open-end solicitation of their points of view.

Quantitative research, on the other hand, "by the numbers," helps both to confirm and tweak your assumptions, a refining of ideas based on statistically meaningful samples.

These are points you consider in detailing and refining the value proposition:

- How much do you really know about current customers? Understanding why your products or services were chosen helps tailor the message. If you don't know, take the time to ask:
  - Why they chose to work with you.
  - How working with you has helped their business.
  - How well they can quantify your value in terms of numbers.
  - What intangible benefits they value.
  - Whether the intangible benefits are important to doing business with you.
  - What they believe your company offers from the standpoint of discernible differences.
  - Whether they would refer you to others.

- Can your current value proposition be evaluated from the potential customer's perspective? Why would anyone buy what you sell? What problems do you solve? What is your solution worth to them? In the past, how have you helped customers:
  - Increase revenue?
  - Avoid costs?
  - Improve profitability?
  - Reduce costs?
  - Improve quality?
  - Retain employees?
  - Shorten product development cycles?
- Research your potential customer's industry for trends. Are you really conversant with the potential customer's world? For example, do you know:
  - What external factors are affecting its business?
  - What is the good news?
  - What is the bad news?
  - How external factors are affecting job roles?
  - What is likely going on inside the company?
  - What are the anticipated needs and pains?
  - What are the company's strengths, weaknesses, opportunities, and threats (SWOT)?

As we have explored, the lead generation program must be in line with the potential customers' buying processes. The attitudes and opinions of these companies are formed long before there is contact with your sales team.

What Is the Customer's Buying Process?

Your way of selling and marketing must conform to the customer's buying process, driven by a clear understanding of needs and the impact of those needs on both that company and its customers. Every potential customer will have a slightly different buying process.

Seminal sales and marketing thinker Neil Rackham, author and creator of *SPIN® Selling*, discovered that all major purchasing decisions go through four distinct steps as illustrated in Figure 5-1:

1. **Recognition of needs.** When the potential customer realizes there is a problem and acknowledges that outside help will be required to solve it, the process of looking for a solution begins with research and gathering of information related to it.

2. **Evaluation of options.** The potential customer, having researched alternative providers, develops decision criteria for narrowing the list.
3. **Resolution of concerns.** The potential customer reconciles the risks and barriers to purchasing, and negotiation of final terms gets started.
4. **Implementation.** The decision to buy is made and the new customer focuses on how the solution will be implemented.[2]

If every potential customer has a slightly different buying process, the physical actions that enter into specifically how the company will buy must be given their due. Just as a seed grows into a tree, so, too, does a customer's need. It is obvious that people cannot be forced to skip steps in their buying process. They buy when they are ready. The need, however, can be fertilized by a well-thought-out value proposition that accelerates the process of lead nurturing. It is much more productive to capture prospects sooner in their buying process than later. Trying to get any meaningful traction with a prospect in its implementation stage will of course be hopeless. However, attention to a long-term future opportunity that meets the ideal customer profile cannot be ignored. As the value proposition is thought through and later in the development of the lead generation program, the key question always is how to capture and understand precisely where the prospect is in its buying process.

2 Neil Rackham, "The Hunt for Growth: New Directions and Strategies for Selling," *Strategy and Leadership*, Vol 25 Issue 3, p 44. Republished with permission, Emerald Group Publishing Limited.

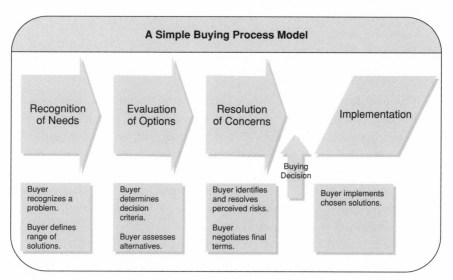

Figure 5-1   Buying process model

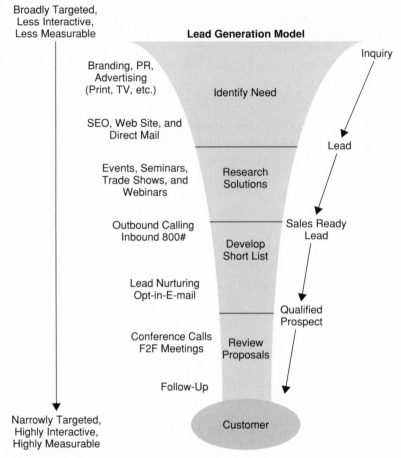

Figure 5-2 Buying process tactics funnel

I have found it helpful to look at the potential customer's buying process on the basis of modalities it employs at each buying step. To that end, the model in Figure 5-2 hypothetically shows the correlation between steps in a prospect's buying process and the sales effort together with tactics that might be of interest at each stage.

The goal is to connect the lead generation modalities and messages with where the prospects are in their buying process. Typically, their reliance will be on modalities they know and trust.

Ultimately, lead generation programs must take into account that your value proposition has to match up with the target's needs and at the right time. Author Kristin Zhivago of *Rivers of Revenue* fame and recognized for creative methods of understanding what buyers are looking for has crafted the concept of a buying process map. The device is designed to help everyone involved agree on how the customer's buying process and the sales team's efforts can be supported in the most productive manner.

Zhivago describes the buying process map as a table that represents the specific steps in a typical sale and who is involved, what the questions are, the answers to the questions, and the marketing and selling tools required to respond. The buying process map is also helpful in selecting the appropriate content for the lead generation plan.

Table 5-1 Buying process map[3]

Intense Scrutiny Buying Process Map
Selling to the point where buyers agree to an ongoing relationship

	Step 1: Getting their attention, bringing in leads.	Step 2: First contact and interaction, answering their initial questions.	Step 3: Meeting: Answering their more specific questions.	Step 4: Proposal, follow-up meetings, calls.	Step 5: Single project test.	Step 6: Agreement for ongoing relationship, close the sale.	Step 7: Ongoing projects.
Who's involved.							
What happens.							
Key buyer concerns at this point.							
Questions they ask.							
Answers that satisfy them.							
Marketing and selling tools needed at this stage.							

3 Kristin Zhivago, *Rivers of Revenue: What To Do When the Money Stops Flowing*, (Jamestown, RI: Smokin' Donut Books, 2004), p 264-265.

Your buying process map can be patterned after similar steps outlined in Chapter 3, Developing the Universal Lead Definition.

As you progress through each of the steps, remember that the key business issues for each individual in the buying process must be understood and addressed. Consistency is the watchword. Each touch, or contact, should add value in its ongoing relevance to the targeted individual, and consistency extends to the style of delivery of the message. Because the sales team is accountable for much of the perception of the company, concerted care must go into helping develop the consistent, relevant communication the sales team will employ in its customer relationship building efforts. Kristin Zhivago writes; "Consistency leads to reinforcement; reinforcement leads to familiarity; familiarity leads to trust. When people have a problem, where do they first turn? To someone they trust. First to their friends, then to the companies they trust."[4]

The objective is to wedge that kind of trust into the affiliation of the salespeople and their economic buyers and influencers. Time and time again it is proven that customers want the salespeople they deal with to understand their business, their needs, and the pressures under which they operate.

Value Proposition by Role

As the value proposition is developed, it is crucial to understand the role of each individual in the potential customer's buying process, which drives the specificity of your message. Figure 5-3 shows some examples of the types of people who may be involved in a typical complex sale situation.

You need to recognize the entire sphere of influence represented by contacts associated with economic buyers, e.g., influencers, information gatherers, opinion molders, and an external sphere of influence represented by end users. All must be addressed with equal intensity. The more you reach the better.

An effective way for developing selling messages is a message map. Message mapping is the development of consistent, well-thought-out messaging that provides the foundation for lead generation programs, marketing and sales messaging, internal tools, and training of stakeholders. The goal is to make it clear to those in the buying process that your value proposition is relevant.

The message map ultimately becomes the preeminent source document of information for communicating with potential customers at various

---

4 Kristin Zhivago, *Rivers of Revenue: What To Do When the Money Stops Flowing*, (Jamestown, RI: Smokin' Donut Books, 2004), p 107.

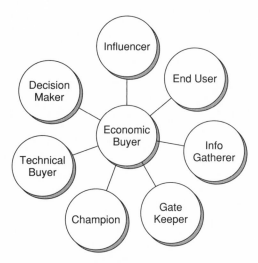

Figure 5-3 Internal sphere of influence

stages. It can be used to integrate situations, instances, conditions, and individuals appropriate to the company and its history into appropriate content for meaningful conversation and directive. It is the guide for developing content for each lead generation tactic.

As we have discussed, strategic collaboration and teamwork are crucial to lead generation success. Refer to the contact roles you captured during the development of the ideal customer profile and the universal lead definition. A brainstorming session with a cross-functional team is an effective method for flushing out all possibilities using such questions as:

- Are you thinking like the potential customer? Develop a profile of each individual who would be involved in the process. Using the ideal customer profile, determine who has a vested place in the sphere of influence. Walk in their shoes. The message map can catalog the pains, issues, trends, and motivations that each customer unmistakably experiences.
- What tangible metrics are used by your existing customers to measure performance specific to your product or service?
- How would your potential customers quantify the value you would deliver?

Further, establish consensus of the marketing and sales teams, including field sales personnel, on your message map and then evaluate, with respect to each individual/job function:

- Issues that are of concern.
- How to respond to issues of concern.
- How the value proposition connects.
- Motivation.
- Who makes the final decision.
- Number of levels to reach in the sphere of influence.
- Language and how they say it.
- Single most important message.

As the message map comes together, imagine yourself as the prospective customer's CEO or other senior management principal. Assume an insider perspective in assessing the company's priorities that will be much more in keeping with the real thing.

I have found mind-mapping to be helpful as a brainstorming device in developing the message map. Mind-mapping, developed in the early 1970s by Tony Buzan, is a method that results in a visual representation of ideas and their connections radiating from a single focus. For example, Figure 5-4 is a message map utilizing a mind map layout.

From that point, create profiles as required. For instance:

- Profile, VP of marketing.
- Business Issue: Concerned about showing tangible return on investment.
- Reason: Unable to provide quantitative financial justification for marketing investments.
- Needs: Consistent feedback from sales organization and ability to track marketing contribution to sales for viable reporting, measurement, and improvement.
- Desired result: Documented return on marketing investment.

Executives are attracted to provocative ideas that can be readily grasped, such as: "Our research shows that 80 percent of the sales leads generated in your industry are ignored. Is this true in your company?"

Follow up with a hard comparison: "It is taking 25 percent longer today to close a sale than it did five years ago, and three more people must be sold in order to close the average business-to-business sale."

Trigger Events in Targeted and Timed Messaging

Any discussion about developing a value proposition must leave room for the subject of trigger events. A trigger event is a happening associated with

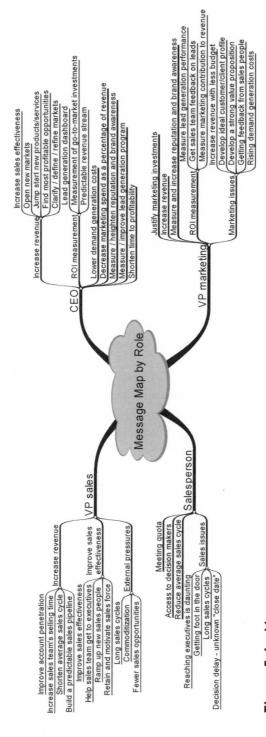

Figure 5-4 Message map

The mind map / message map contains the following:

Message Map by Role

CEO
- Increase revenue
  - Increase sales effectiveness
  - Open new markets
  - Jump start new products/services
  - Find most profitable opportunities
  - Clarify / define / refine markets
  - Lead generation dashboard
  - Measurement of go-to-market investments
- ROI measurement
  - Predictable revenue stream
- Lower demand generation costs
  - Decrease marketing spend as a percentage of revenue
  - Measure / heighten reputation and brand awareness
  - Measure / improve lead generation program
  - Shorten time to profitability

VP marketing
- Justify marketing investments
  - Increase revenue
  - Measure and increase reputation and brand awareness
  - Measure lead generation performance
- ROI measurement
  - Get sales team feedback on leads
  - Measure marketing contribution to revenue
  - Increase revenue with less budget
  - Develop ideal customer/client profile
  - Develop a strong value proposition
- Marketing issues
  - Getting feedback from sales people
  - Rising demand generation costs

VP sales
- Increase revenue
  - Improve account penetration
  - Increase sales team's selling time
  - Shorten average sales cycle
  - Build a predictable sales pipeline
- Improve sales effectiveness
  - Improve sales effectiveness
  - Help sales team get to executives
  - Ramp up new sales people
  - Retain and motivate sales force
- External pressures
  - Long sales cycles
  - Commoditization
  - Fewer sales opportunities

Salesperson
- Meeting quota
  - Access to decision makers
  - Reduce average sales cycle
  - Reaching executives is daunting
  - Getting foot in the door
- Sales issues
  - Long sales cycles
  - Decision delay – unknown "close date"

65

A client that provides enterprise CRM solutions shared this story. According to him, "My group was selling to a company that precisely fit our ideal customer profile and was a qualified lead. We had executive acceptance from the vice president of sales, the vice president of marketing, and had interviewed much of the sales organization. It was down to just two finalists, and we felt we had the edge. Our contacts promised to share their decision with us later in the week. When they called to say we had lost out to a third company, we found it hard to understand why. It turned out that our unknown competitor had developed a close relationship with the CEO via a referral from a trusted consultant, and the decision was made as a result of that. A painful lesson: We had not reached the entire sphere of influence. We missed the CEO and their consulting firm."

a consequence so significant that it causes new behaviors, new ideas, and new opportunities. Trigger events can contribute to the development of timely and relevant sales messages. Let's look at what might be construed as a trigger event:

- New product or service introduction.
- New key hires or recent personnel departures.
- Mergers and acquisitions, corporate restructuring, change of ownership.
- Significant strategic announcements.
- Relocations, office closings, expansions.
- Change in competitive landscape or business climate.
- New laws, regulations, restrictions.

Sometimes identifying appropriate trigger events falls within substantial gray areas. Attempt to sort out what is and what isn't by framing each with:

- What events could happen to fuel interest in and focus on your solution?
- What prompts the urgency to move faster and sooner?
- Which trigger events are relevant to your business and your industry?
- What is an explicit need that could involve your solution?
- What trigger events were evident with existing customers?
- What key words might aid in locating appropriate trigger events on the Internet?

Capturing Real-Time Trigger Events

Information on new business opportunities stemming from trigger events is readily available from libraries, news stories, press releases, news wires, and such specific Internet sources as:

- Technorati watch lists http://www.technorati.com
- Google news alerts http://www.google.com/alerts
- Yahoo! news alerts http://alerts.yahoo.com

In many cases, the alerts and watch list services will send notification to you via e-mail.

Know what is going on in your prospect's business if you intend to address the value of trigger events. Do your homework. Deals may be in the works years before they are disclosed. The key is to develop relationships with the right people long before whatever situations may come to the surface.

Giving credence to trigger events enables the sales team to perform far more effectively. The properly applied and followed trigger event helps shorten the average sales cycle because time is spent connecting with people who have a high likelihood of needing what you have to sell.

We were retained to execute a lead generation program for a product life cycle management—PLM—company. PLM software is used primarily by industrial manufacturing companies to document and support the complete life cycle of their products and to devise and manage ancillary services vis-à-vis product maintenance. The company's sweet spot was the largest product-driven industrial companies whose vice presidents of product development were the most frequent economic buyers.

By plotting out lead generation program results against sales forecasts, we began to see a small group of companies that suggested greater immediacy and dramatically shorter sales cycles. We discovered that on the whole, companies whose CEOs declared greater emphasis on new products publicly were four times more likely to buy the PLM company's solution.

From that point on, the shift was to prioritizing companies that met the ideal customer profile and displayed the obvious trigger event of a CEO who was given to making public new product pronouncements. Sales soared as a result.

The importance of the value proposition cannot be overstated. What else could be said about something that so concisely brings together and proclaims the added worth your company offers its customers and prospective customers? The value proposition is a sustainable action-to-payoff ingredient that today's sales and marketing professionals engaged in actively pursuing new business have less and less latitude to ignore.

Chapter Six:

Building the Lead Generation Plan— Critical Success Factors

No amount of extra time, effort, or budget can make up for a poor lead generation plan. This plan is hardly a blanket marketing campaign. Lead generation requires consistent, sustained, and focused effort for the sales team to sell.

It is not a single-element quest, nor is it an entity solely unto itself. Rather, it represents a long-range commitment on the part of every participant, including those salespeople who might be inclined to give up and move on after an attempt or two. The company that understands this basic truth is miles ahead of the competition.

Marketing professionals, not surprisingly, prefer a strategy-based approach, but when activity is needed *right now* and it becomes a case of ready-fire-aim rather than ready-aim-fire, adherence to a carefully conceived lead generation plan is essential.

A well-executed lead generation strategy can, at the same time, deliver value to the sales team and build a positive reputation with potential customers. To reiterate, teamwork and collaboration are crucial. Before developing the lead generation plan, marketing should integrate its other "customer"—the sales team—into the process.

The plan should clearly define the goals, objectives, strategies, tactics, timetable, measurement, accountabilities, and budget. By their very nature, though, it seems plans are meant to be changed. Should planning therefore be minimized in importance because the market is constantly in flux? Hardly. Just as a guided missile requires programming to hit the right target, so too does lead generation, and the course of both needs minor corrections and adjustments in flight to accomplish its task. Sudden changes in course are generally not tolerated, because just like the missile, a lead generation plan headed in the wrong direction, though launched with good planning, brings a whole lot of trouble.

Lead generation planning must have a focus that is aligned with the sales team's goals. Start by succinctly documenting the common goals, streamlined to fit on a single sheet of paper in the interest of sharp definition and plausibility.

Apply the *SMART* test:

Specific: Exactly what is being sought in terms of actual numerical goals?

Measurable: How will the participants measure their contributions?

Agreed: Do all parties concur on the legitimacy of the target?

Realistic: From past experience, is the goal attainable with present resources and capabilities?

Time: Is the schedule feasible?

Let's examine the process of goal setting more carefully.

Set Goals before Spending a Dime

Before any lead generation plan is put into motion, specific, quantitative goals must be set. Often these are financial goals, and for good reason, but early in the program it will be less than realistic to track financial indicators or performance with sales activity that is only just commencing.

No matter what the goals, they must be in line with and capable of helping drive the corporate strategic objectives.

Number of Inquires and Leads

Goals during early stages of the program should mostly be activity based. If you are overly focused on results-based goals early in the game, you set yourself up for failure. By the very definition of the complex sale, results in terms of sales will not be immediate, nor should they be expected.

When setting goals for sales-ready leads and inquires, it ultimately becomes necessary to take an iterative approach to test and optimize each part of your lead generation plan. That comes with experience, feedback, and results. Start by considering the size of your viable market and match that with your universal lead definition and ideal customer profile. What number of leads seems reasonable?

The number of leads each salesperson can handle during the natural ebb and flow of the sales process is often a barometer of how well the lead generation program is being run. Even the most seasoned sales professional can get too busy to follow up on sales leads. If you are in marketing, don't forget to close the loop with the salespeople. Does their feedback tell you that leads are actually sales ready? Do your universal lead definition and ideal customer profile require adjustment? How many salespeople are there and how many leads can they actually handle? Consider:

- Number of leads required by week, month, and quarter.
- Number of leads required for each salesperson.
- Number of leads each salesperson can manage.
- Number of inquiries required by week, month, and quarter.
- Number of inquiries required for each salesperson.

This information should be captured, written down, and used as a basis to develop your lead generation plan and budget. Because the purpose of lead generation is to help the sales team sell, your lead generation budget should largely be driven by your revenue goals.

Sales and marketing consultant M.H. "Mac" McIntosh has a tool to help calculate the number of qualified leads needed to meet established revenue goals. The Marketing Lead Calculator asks the following:

- What is your company's gross sales target for the fiscal year?
- What percentage of your sales should come from marketing leads?
- What is your average sale size (or the lifetime value of a customer)?
- What is the percentage of sales opportunities your company will win?
- What percentage of your inquiries will become qualified leads?
- What response rate do you expect?
- What are your expected costs per contact?
- How many salespeople need leads?

Communicating the lead generation plan is as important as the strategy itself. The key to success is to develop alignment around your plan first before you launch it.[1]

1 M.H. "Mac" McIntosh, "Free business-to-business (B2B) sales and marketing tools,"< http://www.sales-lead-experts.com/tips/tools/ >, (North Kingstown, RI: Mac McIntosh Incorporated, 2003).

Revenue Targets

Once you are reasonably satisfied with the quantity and quality of your lead generation activity, focus more attention on financial indicators and goals. You quite likely will have financial goals from the outset, especially when selling the program to executive-level customers, but these goals cannot stand as the only determinants of success early on. In some cases, it could be over a year before direct revenue contribution can be measured, depending on sales cycle.

An alternative goal might be to assign estimated deal values to opportunities that move into the sales pipeline. Educated assumptions about ratios can then be applied and revenue projections made. Consider:

- Revenue goal for year and by quarter.
- Sales team, salesperson quotas.
- Revenue value of the sales pipeline.
- Accuracy of sale pipeline—actual deal value and actual sales conversion rate.

Market Share Objectives

If you are in a mature market or a particularly competitive market, you may want to set ancillary goals revolving around market share. These tend to be more difficult to measure but may be useful when new revenue is not a primary corporate goal. Consider:

- Number of new customers measured against your ideal customer profile.
- New segments or industries opened.
- Customer lured away from competitors.
- A successful new product launch.

Return on Investment

It is important to pay careful attention to return on investment goals in your lead generation program. Executives want to know: "What are we putting into this? What are we getting out of it?" ROI goals parallel revenue goals, but they address the additional issue of what the lead generation activity is costing.

Determining return on investment goals is far from an easy matter. It is sometimes necessary, however, to measure it in order to justify continued investment in a project. In smaller organizations it may not be as crucial to know ROI, but larger organizations with top-down controls generally require legitimate, measurable ROI to one degree or another.

To effectively measure return on investment from a lead generation program or activity, leads will have to be tracked from cradle to grave: where the opportunity/lead came from, what happened to it along the way, and its revenue contribution. Additionally, any costs associated with each activity that touched the lead must be known and assessed. For this reason, many organizations outsource their lead generation efforts to better control and measure the expense. If you require accurate ROI measurement, you may want to consider this option.

For accurate measurement of ROI, your marketing database will need to be at a high level of sophistication in order to receive the proper tracking inputs and to generate usable reporting. And, of course, yet again, sales and marketing must be aligned. Without collaboration and buy-in, closing the loop is next to impossible, and so, as a result, is goal setting.

There are important points to have in mind in establishing ROI goals:

- Cost per inquiry.
- Cost per lead.
- Cost per closed sale.
- Lead-to-sales conversion ratio.
- Reduced sales cycle expressed as a percentage.
- Total program cost and revenue contribution expressed as percentage.

As this information is put together, you can begin to develop a goal that meets the SMART goal standard. Here is an example of a goal that was created by a small services firm:

> Our goal is to generate 100 leads and inquires per month, of which at least 20 make it into the sales pipeline. With that in mind, we would expect to bring in two new clients each month, each with average revenue of $100 thousand per year.

Critical Success Factors

Before selecting the tactics you will use in your own lead generation plan, create an outline of the plan itself based on the fundamentals that have been discussed. The following synopsis of critical success factors should be a helpful guideline in establishing the proper mind-set:

Conversations, Not Campaigns

- Aim for relevant and ongoing dialogue.
- Remember that your customer is thinking, "How you sell me is how you will serve me."

- The first impression is a lasting impression.
- Built-in flexibilities allow interaction on a wide range of variables.
- An industry insider posture that says "we get it" reinforces credibility.
- Look for long-term consistency, not the quick hit.
- Effective sales and marketing communication is imperative.

Sales and Marketing—One Team

- All marketing and sales resources are synchronized and collaborative.
- A clearly documented sales process must focus on the customer's buying process.
- Sales and marketing activities are measured and coordinated with shared goals.
- Create value for the prospective customer throughout the process.
- Map tools, skills, and performance metrics with the process.
- Conduct regular feedback meetings for updating and improvement.

The Ideal Customer Profile

- Determine common characteristics among current customers.
- Learn the size of the market and where the sweet spot is.
- Identify decision makers and key influencers.
- Know when to pursue a potential customer and when to walk away.

The Universal Lead Definition

- Inquiries are not leads.
- Establish a clear-cut means of handing off leads to the sales team.
- Don't select leads at the price of quality.
- Define the meaning of sales-ready lead.
- Establish delineation of hot, warm, and future leads.
- Provide only as many sales-ready leads as the salesperson can effectively handle.
- Identify key information for the salesperson to know and use.

The Database

- Use your database as a valuable asset that lines up with strategy and tactics.
- Every inquiry is regarded and protected as vital.

- Track and manage inquiries and leads in a single or logical database.
- All inquiries must be subject to database verification.
- Distinguish between must-have and nice-to-have database fields of information.
- Assign maintenance responsibility and settle on process.
- Keep database current with regular and frequent updates from all stakeholders.
- Ensure visibility throughout the lead hand-off process.
- Determine necessary dashboard reports, e.g.: activity, results, and analysis.

List Acquisition

- Each entry reflects the ideal customer profile.
- Determine and apply appropriate segmenting.
- Prioritize according to perceived potential customer value.
- Include SIC/NAICS codes, revenues, number of employees, other descriptive data.

Value Proposition

- Relevance to targeted prospect must always be in sight.
- Know why a company wants or needs your product or service.
- Messaging from value proposition must be consistent across all points of contact.
- Understand your potential customer's buying process and what stage it is currently at in that process.
- Formalize a concise summation of the value proposition via a message map.
- Research applicable trigger events.
- Systematize trigger events for most effective application and timing.

Multimodal Tactics

- Use a portfolio of appropriate lead generation tactics.
- Assess the number and mix of tactics required.
- Every touch with your customer should represent and communicate value.
- Take a flexible and iterative approach.
- Integrate lead generation tactics together towards achieving optimal ROI.

Effective Lead Management

- Implement and enforce standard universal lead scoring definitions.
- Establish clear process for handling and distributing inquiries and leads.
- Deal with inquiries centrally to prequalify before sending to the sales team as sales-ready leads.
- Identify best opportunities based on application of a consistent methodology.
- Fulfill promised information in a timely manner.
- Assign and define responsibility for lead tracking.
- Track, measure, and report on progress of leads to program close.
- Measure sales performance based on objective criteria.
- Measure sales lead acceptance and follow-up by sales team.
- Define mechanisms and incentives for sales team feedback and updating.
- Measure revenue contribution to drive a faster return on marketing investment.

Lead Nurturing

- Cultivate inquiries to sales-ready leads.
- Motivate salespeople for consistent contact with prospects who may not yet be ready to buy.
- Reprocess inactive leads turned back by the sales team for further attention.
- Pursue and capture future opportunities for nurturing into viable leads.
- Use content to position salespeople as trusted advisors.

The optimal lead generation program involves extensive planning up front with such initial concerns as profile of target markets, identification and analysis of needs, determination of required expertise, and timing. Next, a multimodal integration of tactics and vehicles is required to make it all happen. This multimodal lead generation approach is covered in-depth in Part 2.

Part Two

Lead Generation Tactics for the Complex Sale

Chapter Seven

Synergies in Tactics

No doubt you can describe any number of ways to generate leads for your organization, and quite likely some would produce high-quality, high-value opportunities. Yet for a lot of readers, reaching the upper-level decision makers likely remains their most difficult challenge, regardless of circumstances. To get to these decision makers, an informed strategy is crucial. And the best strategy is one with multimodality and repetition as key elements to improve the odds that those coveted decision makers will be reached.

Although trigger events and timely marketing messaging are key elements for effectively generating leads, dedicated lead generation for the complex sale calls for a comprehensive, disciplined, and multimodal plan of action in order to begin to reach a satisfactory level of return on investment. And naturally, this plan includes full and efficient use of sales productivity and marketing resources.

A multimodal lead generation plan heightens the response rate potential because it more effectively impacts contacts and their sphere of influence. While overcoming the inherent challenges associated with timing, it also enhances audience awareness. One company was able to triple its webinar attendance by a well-thought-out blend of phone calls, e-mail, direct mail, press releases, and Internet communication. Another saw its direct mail response rate exceed 10 percent when phone calls were added to its campaign and a personalized Web page URL was included in the direct mail piece.

One-to-one contact with multiple impressions improves recall and provides a vehicle for building brand awareness and, important to the complex sale, enhancing reputation. According to a Cahners Research study, a typical business-to-business sale that exceeds $35,000 takes an average of 5.12 calls to close. More than 75 percent of companies in the study stated that a sale of more than $35,000 now needs a combination of direct and indirect sales efforts. Over the next five years, businesses believe they will continue to struggle with the ever-increasing cost of closing the sale.[1]

While it may be an obvious statement, it's important to remember that marketers continually strive to get the most for their budget dollars. Lead generation strategies demand results, while at the same time they must be cost-effective. New pressures to generate more qualified leads are giving marketers an added cause to rethink many of their programs. How can they get greater return? Are there allies that have not been recruited? What new tactics can they employ? Marketing people, of course, by virtue of their responsibilities, are forever in search of that single obscure tactic that in and of itself will generate precedent-setting response rates.

Lead Generation Is Like a Financial Portfolio

The CEO who asked his marketing manager about the most effective tactics for generating leads and got the response, "All of them," probably was not too pleased to learn that it takes more than one. How many tactics do you have in your lead generation portfolio?

A client shared this analogy: "I look on our lead generation efforts, particularly in the present economy, as I would a financial portfolio. If I can't measure the tactics or programs in terms of return on invest to the organization—leads generated, business closed, opportunities in the funnel—then why should I expect the company to invest in my fund?"[2] This viewpoint obviously is that of a good financial manager who, needing to draw on resources for new programs over time, maintains an assortment of researched and/or proven best-fit tactics.

Pictured in Figure 7-1 is a mind map showing a vast number of ways to generate leads for the complex sale. This can be downloaded at www.startwithalead.com/resources. As you evaluate it, ask yourself:

- Which of these tactics are we using?
- Which are our competitors using?

Now think of what you know about your prospect's buying process. Is there white space? Where are the gaps?

Most contacts do not become immediate leads, and when the time comes to attempt to land a client, it is wise to have a fallback strategy geared up should it not seem to be going anywhere. The original intent of a phone

---

1 Susan Mulcahy, "Evaluating the Cost of Sales Calls in Business-to-Business Markets: A study of more than 23,000 businesses," (Washington: Cahners Research, January 2002), p 8.

2 Interview with Cheryl Hatlevig, Director of Marketing, Adesso Systems.

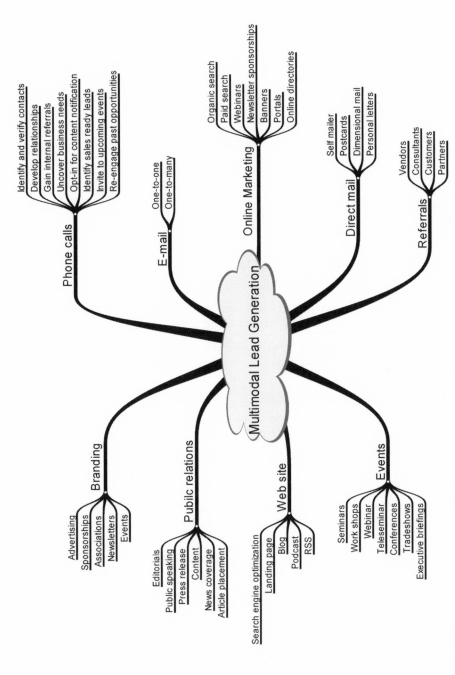

Figure 7-1 Lead generation models

81

call, for example, could be supplemented by an invitation to an event or by mailing relevant information following the call. An invitation to opt-in for an e-newsletter is often effective in priming the pump for bringing the prospect into the lead nurturing program.

The objective of finding an opportunity to get dialogue underway with top executives at prospective companies can be fulfilled in any number of ways. It might be by way of an initial face-to-face meeting, perhaps from introduction by a colleague or mutual acquaintance. Or they may have been motivated in a variety of other ways to make contact with you. Initial dialogue, as many well know, can also be initiated over the telephone under the right circumstances. By whatever means, once dialogue has begun with an actual conversation, the other tactical modes to keep it going—such as e-mail, direct mail, and business events—should be ready and waiting to come into play.

Choosing the Right Tactics

The number of leads converted to sales will rise exponentially once you employ multiple tactics to direct your message to key individuals involved in the buying process. In order that all your potential customers progress to looking at *you* when they are ready to buy, all available tools, smoothly working together, will convey the perception that your interest is personal and relevant—in a very big way.

The multimodal approach calls for a thorough evaluation and systematic planning of your different lead generation methods. Success requires a balance of push tactics that encourages the contact to action and pull tactics that create a strong impression of your company and build brand awareness. Push tactics require communication strategies that are narrowly targeted, such as by telephone, so as to be direct to the individual. Pull tactics are those that include your Web site, which would stimulate the individuals to your whys or wherefores of their own volition.

Think about your prospective customer and the people in the buying process who you most want to reach, the economic buyers. Illustrated in Figure 7-2 are the internal and external spheres of influence that could be surrounding the economic buyer. What tactics would you use to reach the economic buyer through these influencing forces?

It is important to reiterate that the tactics you choose will ultimately help the economic buyers form their opinions, directly or indirectly, as they proceed through the buying process.

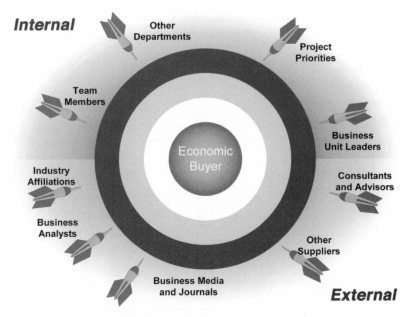

Figure 7-2 Spheres of influence[3]

Table 7-1 can serve as a starter in helping you sort out and identify tactics available for your particular program. And the rest of the chapters in Part 2 of this book will explore in depth the best ways to use each of these tactics.

It is important to note, too, that thinking in terms of multiple modalities for lead generation allows marketing and sales to retrofit revised messaging whenever knowledge about the prospect's position in the buying process is updated. What worked yesterday doesn't necessarily work today or tomorrow.

What exactly does work? Establishing a resilient platform that is adaptable to changes that may be required down the road is always a good place to start. Frequently, lead generation programs don't allow for contingency plans or adequate feedback mechanisms that would foretell the need or opportunity for alteration in the first place. If a tactic fails to deliver, be ready to modify it or replace it.

Try to detail a lead generation calendar for the year that maps out anticipated programs and tactics by quarter. Employ an effective, closed-loop feedback system to structure information from the sales force that can be converted to actionable tactics. (Make it a strong policy to collect sales

3 Figure 7-2. Cheryl Hatlevig, Chris Hawver, *Spheres of Influence*, 2005.

Table 7-1   Lead generation tactics table

Tactic/Purpose	Type	Use it?	Tactic/Purpose	Type	Use it?
Phone call	Push		Blog		
Confirm contact (touch point)			Podcast		
Opt-in for lead nurturing			Really simple syndication (RSS)	Push	
Cross-marketing within customer			Direct mail	Push	
Find immediate leads			Self-mailer		
Clean and update database			Postcard		
Inquiry handling and qualification			Dimensional mail		
E-mail	Push		Newsletter		
One-to-one			Personal letter		
One-to-many			Networking/referral	Push	
E-newsletter			From client		
Public Relations	Pull		Alliance		
Editorial			Channel partner		
News coverage			From friend		
Public speaking			Lead generation content	Pull	
Article placement			Case Study		
Press release			Article (reprint)		
Research report			White paper		
Event	Pull		Research report		
Live seminar			3rd party article		
Workshop			How-to guide		
Webinar			Book		
Teleseminar			Newsletter		
Conference			Success Story		
Tradeshow	Pull		Advertising	Pull	
Web site	Pull		TV		
Search engine optimization (SEO)			Radio		
Pay-per-click (PPC)			Print		
			Sponsorship		

feedback as regularly and as rapidly as possible.) Every available tactic represents an investment, and everyone involved must assume responsibility for maximizing return on that investment to the fullest.

Not only do the disciplined integration and maintenance of a history of touches in the database aid relevancy, they open the doors to tactical personalization. This will give you the ability to tailor the selection of tactics to include the personal touch throughout. Individualized direct mail (such as a desktop-published slick brochure) has been credited with doubling response rates, aided and abetted by a well-structured and effectively employed database.

Iterative Approach with Tactics

Paying particular attention to analyzing, measuring, and optimizing tactics is part of the marketing game. Complacency is not. Well-performing or under-performing tactics should be quickly identified and dealt with accordingly. It is often surprising to suddenly realize how something—or someone—is able to perform better when the most successful tactics are being used. Budget considerations are not exempt. There is close correlation between tactics and budgeted spending, and never should one stray very far from the other.

From the standpoint of cost, quite often the complex sale, even with relatively few orders, pays the marketing bill in short order. But wouldn't it be nice to look into your crystal ball and see the long-term value of a customer and how long it would continue to do business with you? Now that would provide a real basis for determining the most effective spending limits!

From one year to the next or one program to another, lead generation tactics are regularly tested and compared to others to good advantage. Do you know how your tactics are performing? Are they working together in a complementary way to connect each step in the customer's buying process?

By manipulating tactics to perform just a little better, it is hypothetically possible to double the response rate for a program without increasing spending. That said, the appropriate action is to optimize your tactics continuously and incrementally as performance dictates, and not to needlessly spend on methods that are performing below expectations. Don't squander money where it isn't needed.

In reality, sales and marketing—and associated lead generation elements—are essentially processes that can be quantified, measured, and improved. Within these, rating yourself as an operating entity is to seek out and understand your own personal baseline. With a baseline, you can look at how your results differ from your baseline—your variance—and from that determine where you have improved and where you could stand further improvement.

Chapter Eight

The Phone

The phone is one of the key components of the successful lead generation program in context of the complex sale. In fact, to begin a dialogue, phoning is by far the most appropriate and reliable method for contacting high-level decision makers. Phoning is timely, interactive, and personal—the perfect combination of assets for building a relationship. Currently, there are few—if any—viable alternatives to the personal connection and dialogue that you get with phoning.

Even in light of its uniquely important role in the complex sale, phoning cannot stand alone. It must function as the convergence for all other modalities in the lead generation system, the central point for validating and qualifying inquires and leads of whatever description. And no other tool is as accurate when it comes to collecting the qualitative information salespeople require to justify pursuing a lead.

The rules of calling have changed significantly in recent years. It is harder than ever to reach executives on the phone, primarily because in the past pushy salespeople and poorly trained telemarketers tarnished the image of the phone. Also, today's busy executives have less time and more to do, making them highly selective when deciding with whom to speak. This chapter covers effective ways to use phoning as a lead generation tool.

Why Are Salespeople Cold-Calling?

Phone calling is generally the best way to reach an organization's senior executives for enabling dialogue. Unfortunately, the phone is misused and abused by salespeople who do not understand the basic concept and promise of what interactive connection is all about.

Trite but true, the right people have to call at the right time. Forcing highly paid consultative salespeople to pick up the phone and place cold calls

"The deluge of e-mail today has brought a different dimension to phoning. The live human voice makes significant things happen. There is perhaps less economy in a phone exchange than an e-mail message, but economy is not necessarily a good thing when the need is to connect with people. In another sense, phoning implies effort. People appreciate effort. That five-minute conversation requires you to dedicate that much of your time to the person you are calling. You talk. The prospect listens. The prospect talks. You listen. It's an amazing thing, knowing that someone is paying attention and then returning the favor. Amazingly different, anyway.

The voice is the ultimate weapon in the war on anonymity and the best way to create a relationship. If you have a tenuous relationship, if you exchange five e-mails without one live call, if you are dealing with an important issue, or if you are trying to persuade someone of something, invest a few minutes in a live call. On the phone, you have a better chance of hearing the truth, complete with all of those editorial comments and undertones that separate humans from business idiots. If you really want to know, pick up the damn phone."[1]

— Brian Fugere, Chelsea Hardaway, Jon Warshawsky,
Why Business People Speak Like Idiots

is an ineffective—and inefficient—use of their time. But the attitude of "that's what we pay salespeople for" prevails in many companies. The sales team finds itself on a teeter-totter: When prospecting, the board is up and when closing a sale, the board is down.

It is interesting that salespeople are expected to make phone calls but are not always asked to contribute their time to a collaborative lead generation effort. Not only would a salesperson likely turn away from the task of optimizing the corporate Web site or putting together a direct mail campaign, the response would probably be, and not without merit, "Those things would consume valuable selling time, and, frankly, salespeople are skilled at selling, not lead generation, which is someone else's job."

Why, then, in those circumstances, is it that salespeople are expected to use the phone, and only the phone, to generate their own leads? No doubt this stems from an old model of selling in place long before "lead generation"

1 Brian Fugere, Chelsea Hardaway, Jon Warshawsky, *Why Business People Speak Like Idiots: A Bullfighter's Guide*, (Simon and Schuster Free Press, March 2005).

was ever considered a marketing function in its own right, when you simply picked up the phone and called your prospects. The separate and joint efforts of sales and marketing clearly are no longer so uncomplicated, of course, nor should anyone assume that new business is just a phone call away.

It might also be the long-held notion that making phone calls is fairly basic if not easy to do. Everyone has a phone on his or her desk, right? If salespeople can talk to prospects convincingly when face-to-face, why can't they do it over the phone—and throw in lead generation to boot?

Salespeople certainly can speak persuasively on the phone, especially when there has been prior contact and the prospect knows who they are. But that is not reflective of a consistently productive lead generation process. Attempts at phone conversation often fall apart when the salespeople are expected to make cold calls without even the unified and integrated marketing message that the complex sale demands.

Salespeople, it seems, usually do not have the skills or personalities to be teleprospectors, nor should they be expected to spend all of their time on the phone. And they probably do not visualize themselves making phone calls for a living, without direct compensation anyway.

To use phoning as an effective lead generation strategy, consider creating a specialized teleprospecting function within the sales group. Better yet, make teleprospecting a marketing responsibility to create a more direct alignment

---

My company was retained to develop a lead generation program for a client selling exclusively to large firms of at least 1,000 employees. Most of the business came through referrals, but the quantity of referrals was not adequate to meet sales growth objectives.

The new client had developed a preemptive campaign in which its sales team was assigned the task of developing relationships with senior executives through cold-calling. The approach was to invite the prospect to an executive briefing to exchange pertinent key trends with peer companies. After six months, the salespeople had all but given up on the program and gone back to calling existing customers. When the vice president of sales asked why they had quit, it was reported that it was taking from 8 to 12 calls to reach a prospect, and many actually gave up after half that.

It was ultimately concluded that without the skill, desire, and incentive, the sales team should not have been asked to pursue the activity, and a specialized lead generation program was adopted as the result.

with ongoing marketing and reputation-building activities. Many of the steps involved in the conversion of leads to sales can be improved by the contributions of a specialized teleprospecting team. With the universal lead definition and ideal customer profile in force, this team can focus its efforts exclusively on identifying and qualifying sales-ready leads. Salespeople can then do what they do best: sell.

Regardless of infrastructure alternatives, teleprospecting is compatible with the sales personality. Most salespeople are hunters, and many are endowed with the enviable facility for talking the talk and walking the walk. Their dynamic selling and closing skills, however, often require the peripheral help and support of a teleprospecting team.

The telepospecting team must interact closely with the sales team. In simplest form, teleprospectors can turn over qualified opportunities to the field sales team and step aside. It is more effective, despite that, to have teleprospecting support sales throughout the entire sales cycle. Integrating the two through a defined closed-loop feedback process opens up new lead nurturing opportunities.

Although inevitably there will be fallout of sales opportunities from the sales pipeline for one reason or another, rather than allowing them to disappear into the abyss, sales should send these back to the teleprospector so they can be reprocessed as leads. Teleprospectors are then recognized not only as hunters—cold-callers—but also as lead nurturing account specialists, perhaps even as lead management specialists who bring an added element of personal contact to the chase.

As an aside, I am often asked about the proper ratio of lead management to field sales. It is my experience that somewhere between one teleprospector to one or two field salespeople is a good rule of thumb. The lead management team spends about 30 percent of its time on administrative tasks, e.g., updating the database, following up on conversations, and precall research. On average, a full-time teleprospector averages between 40 and 80 calls per day, and of these reaches 8 to 10 true decision makers. They will have talked to many other people, of course, but, we have found it helpful to classify conversations by roles in the buying process, i.e., economic buyer, decision maker, influencer, end user, information gatherer, champion, etc.

Credibly: Telemarketing versus Teleprospecting

In talking with hundreds of executives at midsize to large companies, I find that in terms of calls they receive, the largest complaint is salespeople (and telemarketers) who apparently do little or no research before they make the first call. Many say that the callers "have no idea what our business is" or "they don't understand my role in the company" or "they don't respect my time" or "when I direct them to the right people, they assume I'm lying" or "they don't respect my people." The disgruntled executives also grumble that the caller often wants an appointment immediately rather than at a time convenient for the prospect or demands a large commitment of time or brashly presumes that the prospect is ready to buy. "I feel pressured" and "I feel like prey" are frequently, in no uncertain terms, the result. Scary, isn't it?

The kind of phone abuse that this reflects probably goes back to the time-held view that selling is simply a numbers game, quantity over quality. Selling in the venue of the complex sale is quite the opposite, and the inherent dependence on relationships, insights, and research makes teleprospecting unquestionably a principal tool for establishing competitive advantage.

To set the record straight, by the way, these specialized callers are not the telemarketers that are so vilified in contemporary society. Everyone knows the clichés: Telemarketers read from scripts, their grammar is bad, their insistence precedes them, they call at the wrong times. In effect, they are consummate intruders and bridge-burners. When the complex sale calls for telemarketing, and it does to a degree, the duties of the telemarketer are limited to data gathering and verification that do not require more extensive relationship-building conversations.

Teleprospectors, those in business-to-business marketing, are uniquely different for all the obvious reasons. It is vital that teleprospectors are profiled and employed with the requirements of the complex sale in mind. Though not necessarily critical to relationship-building conversation, they must be smart, articulate, and organized. And their training should focus on making them a consistently productive and sustainable extension of the selling effort.

Outsourcing

Research shows that the addition of an inside teleprospector to support one direct salesperson can increase that person's sales revenue by from 50 percent to 150 percent.[2] Projected, all else being equal, that means that 10 salespeople could end up with as much selling time as 25.

Creating a teleprospecting or lead management team as an internal unit is easier said than done, and frequently it can be downright daunting. Many business-

2 *Inside Sales: Selling More at Lower Cost*, (Stamford, CT: Gartner Inc., 1998).

to-business organizations are therefore outsourcing their phone lead generation activities. Some 729 business-to-business marketers recently voted business-to-business telemarketing as a safest tactic to invest in if they had an extra $50,000 for lead generation.[3] Because chasing executive-level decision makers is the time-consuming task most salespeople dislike, the sales department in most cases is not a logical choice for the function. As one sales manager told me with a chuckle, "90 percent of salespeople hate to cold-call and the rest are lying." In any event, a salesperson selling $2 million annually is worth $1,000 per working hour to the company, and therein is enough reason to look beyond sales.

The next logical question is whether an outside source can adequately generate optimal teleprospecting results for the complex sale. Not outsourcers that deal with transactional sales or low-cost widgets. Rather, if you are considering outsourcing, the goal should be to find savvy, street-smart professionals who specialize in the complex sale and who intimately understand the rationale of quality over quantity in that market. The cost of outsourcing teleprospecting or lead management typically proves to be a very cost-effective $40 to $100 per hour, depending on the usual variables. And often most enticing to marketers is that a comprehensive program can be up and running in less than four weeks.

Under proper circumstances, the specialty business-to-business teleprospecting firm can double the sales team's selling time. My company routinely reports a return on investment of 10 to 20 times for clients as a result of phone-based lead generation programs.

Few salespeople say they are not working harder today than ever before and getting the same or less in return. If you decide to outsource, look for a firm that can partner with your sales force to maximize its efforts while aligning with the company's culture and your value proposition and target market.

If you choose to instead set up your own internal teleprospecting department, remember that a lot of issues must be considered. Ask yourself:

- Do I have support from management to initiate this?
- Does the company have the expertise to build and manage the team?
- Am I in the position to be able to bring in staff?
- Can I identify the necessary talent and specific skills?
- Do I have the resources for extensive training support?
- Do I have space in our facilities for new staff?
- Can I change and/or upgrade our information systems to better manage operations?

3 "Survey Results: If Your CEO Gave You $50,000, What Marketing Tactics Would You Spend it On?" (Warren, RI: MarketingSherpa Inc., May 2004).

- Have I identified overhead and revenue goals?
- Can I afford the learning curve required?
- Do I have sales, marketing, and operations support?

Take the time to assess this fully. Talk to the experts and research both sides, outsourcing and in-house capability. Weigh the strategic issues and determine which alternative best fits your situation.

Using the Phone

If you take for granted that phone calling is a necessary tactic for lead generation today, be sure to not overlook the broader application of the phone for administrative functions in the lead generation program. It is fascinating to see just how versatile—and necessary—the phone is, with such applications as:

- Initial prospecting and qualification.
- Qualifying inquiries from various sources.
- Appending data and information.
- Reconnecting with past customers and leads.
- Centralizing leads for profiling and scoring.
- Following up on requests for information.
- Driving seminar and webinar attendance.
- Inviting and following up on trade show attendees.
- Validating direct marketing lists.
- Following up in direct mail campaigns.
- Building database.
- Scheduling sales appointments.

Overall, four categories of phoning comprise the objectives/application of phoning—verification, qualification, teleprospecting, and nurturing. Let's examine these.

Verification

Phone verification is a fundamental component of the lead generation process and is typically an entry-level function or one performed by someone limited to making telemarketing calls. It is valuable to the early stages of prospecting and throughout lead management, especially if the database is old or incomplete. Verification calling serves the purposes of:

- Cleansing data.
- Verifying contacts.
- Preparing for lead nurturing.

- Increasing targeting accuracy.
- Generating opt-in e-mail.
- Surveying and gathering competitive intelligence.
- Identifying and verifying trigger events.
- Improving messaging for all lead generation modalities.
- Measuring customer service.

Qualification

Qualification calling comes into play when the prospect has "raised his or her hand" but whose demonstrated interest still has not reached qualified lead status. Qualification calling is designed for:

- Preventing wasted time pursuing unqualified leads.
- Ensuring that good sales opportunities are pursued.
- Adhering to the universal lead definition.
- Following up on events.
- Following up on Web site inquiries.
- Following up on all inquiries, regardless of source.
- Following up on direct mail responses.

Teleprospecting

Teleprospecting calls, in the truest sense of prospecting, are those that are employed in the mining of new potential customers who probably have not expressed interest in being contacted and may not even know of your company or what it has to offer. Teleprospecting requires fundamentally sound message and delivery together with the ability to carry on intelligent conversation on the subject at hand. Teleprospecting calls fill the sales pipeline with sales-ready leads by:

- Facilitating outbound teleprospecting.
- Establishing basic lead grading (hot, warm, future).
- Procuring competitive intelligence.
- Setting appointments for sales follow-up.
- Promoting scheduled events.

Nurturing

Phone calling by teleprospectors has a major role in coordinating various facets of the lead nurturing process to ensure regular and ongoing meaningful contact with those classified as nurturing prospects. The more personal nature of lead nurturing often requires that the teleprospector be singularly engaged in reaching specific nurturing prospects on a long-term basis. The inherent complexity of lead nurturing entails phoning to determine and/or facilitate:

- Prevalidating inquiries.
- Verifying inquiries.
- Qualifying inquiries.
- Handing qualified leads off to sales.

The teleprospecting team is also responsible for briefing sales on all inquiries passed over, those that do not come out of the qualification process as sales-ready leads. The importance of this cannot be overemphasized. Keeping everyone in the loop not only helps maintain the collaborative relationship between sales and marketing, but also it emphasizes the value of inquires as latent sales potential.

Cold-Calling with E-Mail

It bears repeating, for the complex sale, the phone is ultimately only as effective as its side-by-side relationship with other modalities. Outbound phone calling and targeted e-mail support one another more productively than any other combination of tactics and remain the best one-two punch for lead generation. The killer integration of e-mail and phone calling has the proven ability to prioritize phone calls in the prospect's mind as the result of the e-mail received beforehand. Keep in mind that familiarity is important. Your efforts will be most effective if the e-mail message comes from the same teleprospector who made the call.

E-mail campaigns in lead nurturing provide tracking logs that reveal what and when prospects clicked on and where they went next. Combined with results of calling and other modalities, the data can be kept in abeyance pending future application.

Peter Davidson, in the "Cold Calling Tips," BeConnected blog, says: "One of the best ways to prequalify your leads is to work off a list of those contacts that have subscribed and clicked through on the content of your e-mail newsletter marketing efforts. Properly written and distributed e-mail marketing campaigns can provide incredibly detailed information and customer intuition that will help your sales staff know what your customers are interested in."[4]

4 Peter Davidson, Cold Calling Tips, BeConnected Blog, (BeTuitive, March 2005), <http://betuitive. blogs.com/beconnected/2005/03/>.

Care, however, must be exercised to not fall back on such information purely because you have it. Relevancy is really the objective. The phone call should parallel the content of the e-mail message. And like with any other attempt, timing is key; the follow-up call must come within a day or two after the e-mail to be truly effective.

Improving Phone Calling Performance

Phone calling's position as an essential element for contact does not guarantee its effectiveness from the standpoint of technique. It has been my experience, however, that the following tricks of the trade can give impetus to better performance:

- **Sustain the calling:** Phone calling in itself is not a campaign, nor is it a quick fix. But sales cycles do require that the lead generation program be long-term and consistent. Investing time and money only to abandon the program in a few months, as too often happens, is an exercise in squandering. Keep it going.

- **Make every call count:** Information is the crux of productive lead generation, and information is what the phone caller seeks. Teleprospectors should be trained not to be quick to terminate the call if the individual being called is not available. Who is to say an assistant might not be helpful? Or that there is not marginal information in the database that should be verified or updated? Or that referral to an alternative decision maker would not be appropriate?

- **Scripts and call guides:** In the simplest of terms, the telemarketer reads from a script and the teleprospector follows a call guide. Scripts can be good. In their setting, they promote messaging consistency, are efficient, and help ensure that elements of the call are not overlooked. Scripts, though, leave little room for conversation. Call guides, whose primary objective is to perpetuate a conversation, do not score a presentation verbatim. They are instead an outline of areas to be discussed and questions to be asked. They are built for flexibility and assume a variety of outcomes while still promoting consistency and relevancy of message.

- **Top-down:** Be mindful of the fact that it is better to be referred down than to be referred up. While high-level executives may be difficult to reach, they can in fact be accessible, and the effort must be made. The option of being referred to a subordinate is sometimes just fine; referral from on high to a subordinate often opens very favorable dialogue.

- **Executive assistants are allies:** The executive assistant should not be looked on as a barrier to initiating dialogue. On the contrary, executive assistants frequently occupy a significant place in the sphere of influence and are keenly aware of corporate issues. Don't be afraid to develop a relationship with people titled "assistant."
- **Be relevant and informed:** In the complex sale, the stakes are too high to preemptively call someone who the caller appears to know nothing about. It needs to be obvious that the caller has a sound working knowledge of the potential customer—and the company—and understands the issues faced. The credibility of conveying with confident assurance a personal interest in the prospect goes a long way towards establishing meaningful dialogue.
- **Align teleprospectors with verticals and roles:** To speak with credible relevance regarding the subject at hand, the teleprospector's assignment should be confined, if feasible, to a narrow selection of industries or vertical markets. There is thus greater familiarity with the ins and outs of the business and a sense that "these people know what they're talking about." The same is true with each role in the buying process. Do you portray that you understand their world? Do they feel you get it?
- **Gain opt-in:** As a matter of course, when speaking with a prospect it is judicious to request permission to e-mail subsequent helpful information. More often than not, the answer will be in the affirmative, thus affording you another building block for staying in touch. Of course, it is crucial that you follow up in a way that is precise in terms of promptness and relevancy.

Though phoning takes the lead in tactical choices for identifying potential customers and initiating and maintaining dialogue that will bring them to the position of sales-ready leads, it is only as good as the synergy it creates in combination with other tactics or media towards that end.

Chapter Nine

E-Mailing with Credibility

Universally, marketers love to use e-mail marketing for nurturing and cultivating future opportunities with target audiences. E-mail has earned the much-sought label of *cost-effective*. For perpetuating dialogue, e-mail is probably the most cost-effective medium there is.

Yet e-mail is also a source of stress for many executives—as it is, unfortunately, for many of us. Most are quite simply overwhelmed by the proliferation of spam. And dozens—sometimes hundreds—of sales and marketing e-mail messages make their way to executive mail boxes each day. Some are mildly interesting, but most lack in any meaningful kind of relevance. E-newsletters fall right in there, oftentimes as little more than nuisance mail. In the end, executive recipients just don't have time to read much if any e-mail, good or bad.

So, if in theory e-mail is good for building trust, how can it be tailored to do that in practice? How can you ensure that it will be read in the first place? To start with, pay heed to the principle that less is more. Creatively concise, to-the-point messaging wins over wordy broadsides that are likely to elicit a quick delete even before they are read. E-mail rules have changed accordingly. Whereas it was once asked:

- How do I build my opt-in list?
- How big is my list? Can I make it bigger?
- How good is my subject line?

It is now:

- How effective is my relationship-building?
- How many contacts within my sphere of influence do I have on my list?
- How relevant is my e-mail messaging?

Push Content, Not Graphics

There is no doubt; e-mail is a great way to build on conversation and continue the dialogue. For lead generation, e-mail is a one-to-one medium, nothing more, nothing less. The objective is to take full advantage of the unique characteristics of e-mail in creating meaningful communication that is at once attention-getting and informative—in a style easily perceived to be directed exclusively to me, the recipient.

Good e-mail context is brief and clearly dedicated to the business at hand. It is not glitzy with graphics or entertaining with special effects. If anything, it has the appearance of being hand-typed by the sender, which evokes the personal touch. For the sake of brevity of the primary message, attendant or complementing information can take the form of an attachment or hyperlink reference. Examples:

- By-lined articles.
- Third-party articles relating specifically to your value proposition.
- News releases, news stories.
- White papers.
- E-newsletters.
- Event invitations (e.g., seminars, webinars, executive briefings).
- Research reports.
- Survey results.

Development of an effective e-mail program depends on how much you know about your target audience. And on the comprehensive database that is valuable in working the campaign through the stages of the buying process. Knowing your target audience and where you are in the buying process at any given time is a wonderful combination that can guarantee the relevance of each and every e-mail sent.

Templates

Situational e-mail templates are exceedingly helpful to the sales team. Although some companies have done this successfully, asking people participating in the lead generation process to compose individual messaging from scratch can actually be harmful because it creates a discord in the consistency of your messaging. E-mail templates obviate this problem by underwriting the all-important consistency of message and orientation with strategy.

Templates enable users to modify and personalize the message to fit the occasion while keeping a consistent message. Teleprospectors should have a catalog of e-mail templates that give them the latitude for timely response to particular situations while remaining within the parameters of the program. In addition to the templates, marketing should also be able to supply collateral materials such as case studies, white papers, et al. that could be incorporated to enhance the e-mail. In developing templates, pay close attention to your message map for consistency of targeting and message. A list of suggested e-mail templates could be endless. Here are a few:

- One that would be directed to motivate the executive's assistant.
- One that would inspire the recipient to request more.
- One that outlines the logical steps expected of the dialogue process.
- One that invites the recipient to a special event.
- One that touches base with a contact not recently approached.

In the broad view, an e-mail campaign demands that you:

- Review all interactions and contacts with the company for relevancy of message.
- Get the contacts' permission and document in the database how they chose to opt-in.
- Strive for good first impression with creativity on the subject line.
- Consistently send from the same person until the qualified lead has been handed off to sales.
- Create personal relationships by way of the personal touch.
- Provide useful and educational information in tone and content
- Integrate the e-mail system into the database for centralized organization.
- Solicit advice from existing customers or subscribers on appropriate e-newsletter topics.
- Refrain from overwhelming prospects by trying to sell directly.
- Promote your Web landing page in e-mail.
- Capture actionable e-mail tracking data.

Building the E-Mail List

Many marketers have encountered difficulty creating an opt-in e-mail list. Here are a few ideas that have been shown to alleviate the common problems they encounter:

- The opting-in proviso is fundamental to the lead generation calling program, and sales people or teleprospectors should always request opt-in permission to send relevant information.

- Add enticements to learn more on the Web site landing page.
- Add a sign-up or registration form to your Web site with a hyperlink to the company's e-mail privacy policy.
- Add a separate check box for newsletter signup to the Web site contact-us form.
- Establish incentives for the prospect to provide contact details when requesting available white papers, reports, case studies, etc., together with an opt-in check box.
- Put e-newsletter archives online for easy access via search engines, indexing relevant content.
- Include messaging that provides a link to your e-newsletter.
- Offer various available collateral materials by an opt-in check box.
- Promote your e-newsletter by all available means at events or on webinars, etc.

Executive Reach

If targeting executives is one of your biggest challenges, try one of the following proven ways to get their attention:

- Use e-mail follow-up to a phone conversation to reinforce what was discussed.
- Extend the invitation to a breakfast roundtable with peers and a speaker.
- Extend the invitation to a webinar relative to industry or job function.
- Send an e-mail message of congratulations or compliment on recent media attention.
- Provide information from studies and research on key business trends relevant to industry or job function
- Strike the right balance in terms of frequency. Too many e-mail messages can be as ruinous as none at all.

E-mail marketing is a useful tactic for lead nurturing and relationship building, but the only way to effectively sustain a dialogue is to use it in conjunction with precisely accurate data from a well-integrated database. Conversely, no one needs the embarrassment of assailing important prospects with uninformed, erroneous information. Further, with today's increasingly complex technology, many companies are finding it effective to retain professional service firms to manage their e-mailing campaigns. When outsourced, e-mail is often more cost-effective, and the pitfalls of unenlightened e-mailing techniques are minimized.

A fast-growing consulting firm was doing a lot of things right—except for e-mail marketing. As a high-level financial consulting company, it offered complex projects such as premerger due diligence and postmerger integration. The indiscriminate e-mailing it practiced bombarded potential clients, mostly CEOs, weekly with routine, pointless messaging. It started receiving a lot of negative feedback. The CEO/recipients had opted to receive e-mails from this company because information it offered was good and it was valuable. Now, because of the onslaught of e-mail for the sake of e-mail, they were inclined to want out. Enough was enough. Eventually the company's credibility and image were chipped away by a poorly conceived e-mail campaign. With better concept and frequency, the results would have been quite the opposite.

E-mail can be used to nurture leads and customers. The following is an example of one company that segments its database by territory so that prospects and clients get their own individual salesperson's smiling face on e-mail messages.

A large company providing outsourced energy management solutions for major energy users took tentative steps to begin sending an e-mail newsletter to executive prospects on behalf of each salesperson. At first the salespeople resisted; there was concern that the prospects might take exception. All the same, the campaign moved forward with the assistance of a core sales group. The e-newsletter itself featured a photo of the respective salesperson in a pointedly personalized format and with quite appropriate and informative content. Recipients liked the approach, compliments began to reach the participating salespeople, and the e-newsletter gained wide popularity.

Soon the culture of the company shifted to a sharply focused e-mail m.o. The sales team now feels this is one of the best things it has going for it, and permission has been procured to regularly announce new services and other information pertinent to possible future business.

Why did it work? They turned something typically viewed as mass medium (which e-mail is not) into a personal touch from a real human being.

Other E-Mail Considerations

For the complex sale, the purpose of e-mail should be less about creating leads and more about continuing a meaningful dialogue. Leads are ultimately realized only if the communication becomes two-way. E-mail tracking is important in the continuing attempt to generate meaningful dialogue.

Adding e-mails to the database offers results not always available by sending e-mail alone. Many database and CRM solutions now contain such e-mail marketing tools as e-mail template creation, reporting and tracking, permission management, and deliverability management.

Whether they are generated from an outsourced vendor or from in-house support, the details you receive from an e-mail campaign should be added to your database as a matter of course. The ability to use e-mail tracking data and capture e-mail-generated behavior is invaluable to the sales team.

It is not enough to know that someone clicked on an e-mail URL definitively or even opened an e-mail a number of times; the indication you are looking for is that someone actually responded. Or didn't. The goal then is to capture the nature of the response and the WHO if there was one and add it to the record for later reference as the lead generation effort continues. The value of this to the salesperson can't be overstated, and what better place to look for it than a well-maintained database.

Marketers are learning to develop tools that connect with the database and that provide all manner of relevant data to their salespeople on a regular basis. They build in a process that recognizes when a recipient has clicked on a link to download a white paper, is reading your e-newsletter, or has participated in a recent webinar. This is all good and potentially priceless knowledge as the relationship with the contact evolves.

Filters can be created that enable focus on records showing particular e-mail activities, thus providing flagged reminders for appropriate and timely follow-up. Calls should be especially subtle from a trust-engendering standpoint. For example, instead of saying "I'm calling because I see you've read our last white paper a dozen times," use an approach that poses the question in a restrained way to determine whether the individual or company has an interest in the related subject.

Because of the proliferation of spam-filtering software, even personal opt-in e-mail messages do not necessarily get through to the target. Deliverability management tools help test the e-mail templates to ensure they don't trigger a false-positive at the point of filtering and still be compliant with governmental regulations.

Personalization

Every member of marketing and sales desires a customized message that will make the best impression on potential leads and that allows the lead-nurturing process to begin. You can create this message by building in your database a system that supports sending personalized messages and merging data from a source record. The e-mail campaign system should offer but not necessarily be limited to such personalization options as vertical industry, region, company size, and job function.

Personalization can be triggered by any field in the database, and database options may be selected for:

- Creating a seminar invitation, precompleted with contact information of record, with a link to a sign-up Web page.
- Originating the message "from" the sales person directly involved with pursuing the prospect.

Figure 9-1 illustrates one basic approach your e-mails might take.

Use the following checklist as a guideline when developing your e-mail campaigns:

- **Define the goals.** Build the relationship by sharing useful, educational, and relevant information or request such actions as reading a

---

To: (Recipient)

From: (Sender)

Subject: (Article) "Why Marketing and Sales Can't Seem to Co-exist"

(Recipient's first name),

After our call, I thought you would be interested in this article. No doubt, like the rest of us, you have had to confront this situation. (www.samplelink.com)

Also, here's another article, "Getting Sales and Marketing on the Same Team," that purports to bring a solution to the problem. (www.samplelink.com)

If you have related needs or would like to discuss the articles, please give me a call at 651-555-0000 or reply back.

Have a great day!

Thanks and regards.

Figure 9-1   Example e-mail

proffered article or white paper, registering for a webinar, or participating in a peer survey.

■ **Define the audience.** Determine if you are targeting a narrowly
defined, customer-based segment or the entire house list and identify
the recipients and what is important and relevant to them.

■ **Define the message.** Conclude how and in what order to describe the
benefits of the offer.

■ **Define the vehicle.** Evaluate communication alternatives; determine
whether an e-newsletter, a one-to-one letter, a one-to-many letter, or
something else is indicated.

■ **Define the delivery timing.** Resolve when the audience is most likely
to open and read the e-mail message, i.e., day of the week, time of day.

■ **Confirm that:**
  ● The "from" line contact name matters. Is the message from a name
    they already know?
  ● The "subject" line is accurate and effectively brief and to the point.
  ● Format and content are properly personalized.
  ● Copy is clear and concise.
  ● Copy is free of words that offend spam-triggering filters.

■ Before implementing:
  ● Proofread the entire e-mail communication and then proofread it
    again.
  ● Verify all links for veracity and functioning.
  ● Preview and test-send the e-mail in HTML and text.
  ● If you are doing this on behalf of your sales team, be sure that each
    salesperson has pre-approved sending e-mail to that specific con-
    tact; you can give salespeople "Do Not E-Mail" flags in your data-
    base or CRM to facilitate that. Ideally, any e-mail replies go to the
    sales person directly. If that is not possible, then forward all rele-
    vant replies to the appropriate person ASAP. Be sure to alert sales-
    people when an e-mail campaign goes out to their contacts.
  ● Finally, consider that the e-mail must look personalized. It should
    be devoid of corporate speak. It's about being real.

E-mail as a significant element of doing business today looks past conventional thinking and pays little attention to the status quo. If executed
carefully and within the demands of the complex sale, e-mail is a technology
that has few equals for helping pave the way to more productive relationship
building. Next we'll explore the role of public relations in lead generation.

Chapter Ten

Public Relations
and Lead Generation

The simplistic view of public relations is that it is a device that promotes goodwill through the media coverage it acquires. While that might be an acceptable viewpoint in some quarters, today's public relations—PR—is actually a major instrument in the lead generation process.

Public relations is the function of communicating your company's image and brand to a target audience in a deliberate, planned, and sustained attempt to create and maintain mutual understanding. It should not be confused with publicity, which is just one of the methods used in communicating image.

A recent survey reveals that sales and marketing disagree on the real worth of public relations. The PR firm SHIFT Communications found that 37 percent of survey respondents believe lead generation is an essential function of PR, yet 49 percent said the best measure of PR success is the generation of more or better sales leads. A greater number of respondents, 74 percent, believe PR and word of mouth are more effective than advertising at generating sales leads.[1] The survey concludes that sales leads from PR are highly valued but not expected due to the lack of data, the methodology, and cooperation needed to easily make the PR/lead-generation connection.

Lead generation for the complex sale relies less on PR for developing product or service brand than it does on focusing squarely on building reputation. When you think about it, the discipline of lead generation is a measure of status and character, at least in the game of business-to-business marketing, and that translates into corporate reputation. The objective is not to promote brand awareness to the end-use consumer in the traditional sense

1 "Launch Pad Survey on PR Perception Gap," (SHIFT Communications, 2004).

(think Coca-Cola), but rather to publicize the corporate brand whose image of trust and relevancy enables differentiation from other firms, suggesting value. In short, a good reputation leads others to make conclusions about the corporate brand, but the corporate brand itself does not create reputation. Reputation comes alive for business-to-business companies in the areas of demand creation, lead generation, and overall revenue growth.

SiriusDecisions, a leading business-to-business research firm, says it best: "While brand isn't dead, we believe it has become a byproduct of reputation, the first of three overall outputs today's business-to-business organizations must systematically produce in order to be successful. Reputation has a direct link to the second output—demand creation—and indirectly helps to drive the third—revenue—by building a foundation of trust and credibility that should be revisited as needed throughout a sales cycle."[2]

The public relations effort designed on behalf of a lead generation program therefore focuses on reaching the target audience and its sphere of influence with the notion that your company can be a productive business partner.

When Is PR Required?

Sometimes nothing more than a gut feeling dictates the necessity of a public relations move; if it seems right, do it. But PR is more successful when it is carefully thought through. PR is an enormously disciplined marketing tactic, a "pull" mechanism that requires a consistent and sustained commitment to be successful. Lead generation tools like webinars, e-mail campaigns, and telephoning are inherently more effective if there already is a positive perception in the minds of the contacts. PR can help influence the decision by instilling that positive perception directly and by spurring collateral campaigns to achieve faster results.

PR is still often misunderstood among executives; some of them have always held the general belief that PR is great for propagating free advertising. Hardly. Good PR, including but not limited to well-composed and distributed press or news releases, requires concerted time and effort to establish your company as the go-to source for the solutions they need. The process of building relationships with the media and with analysts is just as demanding as nurturing and cultivating relationships with prospects. The innumerable aspects of the study of public relations are readily available in texts and articles

2 "Graduating From Brand to Reputation," Perspectives, SiriusDecisions, March 2005.

dedicated to the subject. Our goal here is to suggest how you might better position your company—and therefore improve your lead generation processes—as a recognized expert with the help of PR and PR-related tools.

You as a Thought Leader

Your professional expertise gives you and your company a leg up in combating commoditization. You still have to plant your expertise and specialization in your prospects' minds by proactively gaining a reputation for it. You want to evolve into a company that is a renowned expert at providing value instead of being just another firm selling products or services. As a recognized expert—or thought leader—customers and potential customers will respond to you or seek you out when a solution is called for. The term "thought leader" is only as good as the people filling the office, but given the right raw material, the reputation for quality and value can be built with meaningful PR efforts.

> One company that does CRM consulting positions its principals as thought leaders. Or that is what they call themselves on the company Web site. Yet under the Web site heading "Thought Leadership," there is nothing more than mention of a few available white papers, blatantly requiring registration in order to download. Neither through their Web site nor in the company's presentation is there any proof that supports their claim of being thought leaders. Not very well done. And not very good public relations.

Ultimately, a truly legitimate thought leader is a person or company that has earned the reputation as *the* recognized authority in a specific field. The recognized authority part of it comes from an outside assessment based on what others say about you, not what you say about yourself, and properly created and properly executed PR must always take that into account.

According to Elise Bauer of Pacifica Group Management Consultancy, "What differentiates a thought leader from any other knowledgeable company (or individual) is the recognition from the outside world that the company deeply understands its business, the needs of its customers, and the broader marketplace in which it operates. Trust is built on reputation, and reputation is generally not built on advertising or looking smart."[3]

There is no question that potential customers readily pick up on something that isn't genuine. Their sense of the disingenuous seems to have

3 Elise Bauer, "Be A Thought Leader!," On the Job Blog, 10 November 2003.

mythical proportions to some. The thought leaders who are less than mag-nanimous about creating, advancing, and sharing ideas with others are soon found out, and with someone like this, no amount of hype is going to paint a picture of a person who is investing in helping potential customers.

Increasingly, the many new ways that such things become visible are rap-idly putting entrepreneurial young companies closer to equal footing with their larger counterparts. Elise Bauer adds, "Become a thought leader in your field and it won't matter as much how big you are. Companies and people will look to you for insight and vision. Journalists will quote you, analysts will call you, and Web sites will link to you." This, in turn, becomes the stuff of PR that is searched for and that ultimately builds your reputation and brings customers to you.

Thought Leaders in Lead Generation

Real thought leaders communicate; they write, they speak, and in many ways they openly share insightful ideas. They create content, and content is king in the knowledge management realm. All kinds of content can be creatively exercised to position your company as expert. Not only is thought leadership then demonstrated, but new appreciation exists that there is genuine regard for the prospect's well-being.

To help position you or your company as a thought leader, the content you provide should be:

- Germane to the target audience or its sphere of influence.
- Timely in addressing the issues of the target audience.
- Clear in demonstrating value and ties to the value proposition.
- Able to portray value at first glance.

Modalities for sharing, promoting, and distributing content depend on the market. As a general rule, try selecting less-intrusive methods of captur-ing the attention of those who have not gotten past the awareness phase. More intrusive means are for determining the prospect's status as the process evolves and how you might better serve. This also can vary by role and tim-ing. The advantage to this approach is that by creating content that engages potential customers early in the buying process, they are brought into the lead-nurturing program, enabling good timing of relevant information that casts you in the role of resource or trusted advisor and positively impacts the program.

The thought leader mind map in Figure 10-1 illustrates content that could conceivably position your company as expert. To be thought of as an

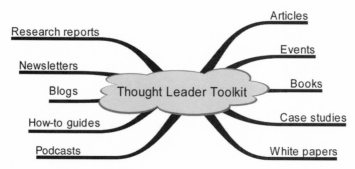

Figure 10-1   Thought leader toolkit

expert, it must be sharply apparent that your thought leadership skills reflect the potential customer's needs, issues, and concerns. The following sections discuss specific ways to establish yourself as a thought leader.

Public Speaking

Speaking publicly as an expert or authority figure can be instrumental in the development of a considerable amount of credibility. Many companies market a product or service so complex that their value proposition must be "unpackaged" publicly now and then to prevent it from being overwhelming to potential customers. Speaking in public is less about selling what you do than it is selling what you know. The knowledge you impart as an established expert is what prospects take back to their specific situations.

Such events as live seminars, workshops, webinars, and conferences provide the forum and the opportunity for beneficial publicity. While people who want to learn something from you are attracted to these events, many times they represent a narrow audience like existing customers or prospects already familiar with you. To increase exposure and bring in new blood, however, it is necessary to be proactive in seeking broader opportunities through industry groups, associations, or academic institutions. Also, firms specializing in public relations and speaker placement and management can be of ongoing help in securing appearance opportunities.

To get in touch with the "speaking circuit:"

- Determine where your target audience might be concentrated with information from your ideal customer profile.
- Develop a topic based on your value proposition map that focuses on appropriate pain, solutions, trends, etc.

- Select who from your organization should be the speaker: in smaller companies, perhaps a senior executive positioned as a thought leader or expert; in larger companies, anyone from senior down to director level staff.
- Be creative in developing content that is educational and take-away valuable.
- Take the time to research who and what have been presented to the group before to confirm that it is in fact your target audience.
- Gain familiarity with the group's calendar and its scheduling requirements.
- Get to know the organizers and their criteria and process for evaluating potential speakers.
- Develop a proposal for the appearance and follow-up that express best interest in the audience.
- Consider comarketing, sponsoring, or promoting the event, and show how easily it can be marketed.
- Persevere; if at first you don't succeed . . .

Working with and appearing before an independent group often results in pre- and postevent media coverage. This can mean more attendees. And it is undeniably important that the event be promoted.

Inquiries collected at or generated by an event are gold. Inquiries can be promoted by having handouts available, reprints of pertinent articles, white papers, case studies, newsletters, e-newsletters, and such information as a dedicated URL referral or your Web site landing page for embellishment. Provide a means for speaker evaluation with an opt-in "subscribe me-call me" space. The ultimate objective is to translate interest into meaningful opportunities that will encourage further conversation towards the reward of lead qualification.

Relationships developed in speaking before independent groups invariably help increase the odds of editorial coverage of the individual or company as time passes, if for no other reason than the process of association. Reporters/editors regularly rely on trade sources of all kinds for news, and why not you, too, as someone who represents a connection?

Getting Published

Visibility is the key watchword. Towards that end, it is to your advantage to have an article placement strategy that is underwritten by the creation, circulation, and availability of by-lined news releases and published articles. These should always speak to your value proposition. Building a library of content takes time, but the value of such things in developing you or your company as thought leader and trusted advisor is immeasurable. Again, the goal at any given moment should be to provide relevant subject materials that most properly fit an ideal customer profile and the sphere of influence.

We have previously examined the concept of developing the value proposition by interviewing current customers and asking where they traditionally get information related to their professions and businesses. To get the best visibility, it's important to have a working knowledge of the most-followed publications and other news sources in your area of expertise. This knowledge is valuable for reaching existing customers and potential customers alike, with targeting background gleaned from:

- Most credible print, broadcast, online media, and blogs.
- Specific media most regularly followed.
- Type of information sought or relied on from each medium.
- Trade group or association memberships.
- Current market information in circulation.
- Trends and news from the field via the sales team.

Knowing what your customer regularly reads will make it easier for you to search out topics of interest that are related to the value proposition. Another smart strategy is to establish relationships with editorial personnel at the most appropriate media. This tactic will ultimately create visibility for the prospects you most want to reach.

The content of your PR efforts can be viral; if people like what you say or what you are represented as saying, they will pass it along. In short, good content spreads. It is good to look at some suggestions on sharing your content, such as:

- **The sales team.** Salespeople are able to employ bragging rights credibly, allowing them to work complimentary editorial mentions into their conversations as relevant.
- **Press releases.** The media are always on the watch for news.
- **Online publicity tools.** Consider using these low-cost mechanisms of publishing content for PR: blogs, RSS (Really Simple Syndication), online press release distribution, and podcasting. These tools allow journalists and the public at large to get the material they want, rather than sending huge amounts of e-mail to people whose in-boxes are already overcluttered.
- **Online search engines.** When posting content on your Web site, include a detailed summary that will enable search engine indexing.

- **Reprints.** Advertising, articles, or editorial mentions should be reprinted in quantity and used diligently for personal handout, direct mail distribution, press kit, and Web site response purposes.

Improved Web Site Visibility and PR

People may be attracted to your Web site for a number of reasons, and no doubt you want it to be known as a source of good, solid, easily accessed information about your company or industry that fits the needs of your customers. As a device for publishing information dedicated to your cause, the Web site is without parallel. Developing a profound awareness of your Web site should take into consideration such precepts as:

- Search engines are crucial, and with focus on content, keywords, linked external pages, and bearing on the topic, they can point an interested party directly to your Web site.
- Posting articles on the Web site increases relevancy and the likelihood that your site will turn up in response to searches on online search engines.
- The Web site ultimately makes you a resource with the continuing demonstration that there is much to be gained from your expertise.
- Carefully observe the fine line between providing content for download at no charge and protecting it by requiring registration.

Your potential customer is deluged by countless and fragmented information streams. Strive to employ PR in its many forms to reach these prospects and increase the probability that your lead generation programs will succeed.

The PR strategy is built on long-term vision. It may seem that you are investing an inordinate amount of time and funds without much immediate payback, especially when the demand always seems to be for more sales-ready leads *now*. Reputations do not happen overnight, however, and it is good to remember that public relations is in essence a sustained effort over an extended period of time.

Chapter Eleven

Event Marketing

Although it's hard to understand why, some marketers seeking new venues tend to shy away from event marketing as a lead generation building activity because of the notion that certain aspects make events a dicey venture. Many worry, "What if no one shows up?" Or, "What if the program falls flat on its face?" Or, perish the thought, "What if we don't get satisfactory results or ROI?"

At a basic level, an event is something that happens at a given place and time. Which events you will favor will depend on what you are selling (how complex is it?) and your target audience. Most events fit into categories: promotional driven or reputation driven.

Promotional, i.e., branding, events may include sponsorships such as NASCAR, PGA Golf Tour etc. The objective is name recognition and association. Branding events are used more often by marketers, where you are looking to influence the perception of a larger audience.

Reputation-building events take promotional events to the next level. They may include seminars, summits, symposia, trade shows, or conferences with current or potential customer invitees focusing on content designed to improve sales or customer relations. These are actions for business-to-business and business-to-consumer marketers with a more complex sale.

Events are a highly visible way to demonstrate your marketing prowess. Or the lack of it. Beyond the fact that it is more difficult than ever to attract people to live events, the events themselves require a large amount of careful planning and development, good content, and great orchestration.

The truth of the matter is, though, event marketing can deliver a quite impressive return on your lead generation investment.

I give a lot of attention to the value of webinars, which are currently the champion of event lead generation tactics. Webinars are relatively inexpensive compared with traditional in-person events and are an attractive tactic for marketers trying to reach busy prospects who can't or won't leave the office. It should be pointed out, however, that much of what goes into a webinar is relevant to conventional live seminars and public speaking opportunities as well. Regardless of the type of event, be aware of how your content should be tailored to appeal to attendees at different stages in their buying processes.

Content Is King

There is little chance of getting—or at least holding—people's attention without knowing where their interests lie. You already know what your prospects are looking for. You have identified, initiated, and nurtured relationships with them. Now it is time to think in terms of what you can provide that they can't easily get anywhere else. For your event, what are you going to talk about? What is your positioning? What is your messaging? What are the hot topics?

To uncover what your customers are interested in, look to a variety of sources available to you, including feedback from other interfaces, editorial cues, trade journal lowdown, industry intelligence, whispered tips, and your sales team's input. Or relevant content for development of timely topics from white papers, articles, research reports, surveys, and case studies. Do, though, always keep in mind that the best choices are those that most closely align with your value proposition.

The last time you scrutinized a reference book in response to a particular issue, you probably gained some practical insights that you put to work right away. Very simply, you made a good investment of time and effort, and it felt good, similar to the satisfaction you ultimately want to instill in your event audience with appropriate, interesting, and credible content. Let's examine where to use this content most effectively.

Webinars

The newest device in the business-to-business marketer's toolbox and especially effective for advancing lead generation dialogue is the webinar. A webinar is basically a seminar conducted over the Web. In contrast to a webcast, which transmits information only in one direction, a webinar enables interactive exchange between the presenter and the audience. It is live according to an agenda, and the presenter speaks over the phone about information that is simultaneously presented on the screen to which the audience may respond. The webinar is a powerful medium for communicating with potential customers and nurturing leads, qualified leads, and current customers.

Webinars, however, look easier to put together than they are. The high frequency of webinar use today dictates that production as well as content be increasingly unique and thought provoking in order to attract participants. Your prospective customers, who are probably bombarded with webinar invitations from other companies, will discriminatingly pick only those events that are compelling and potentially insightful to them. Hence, if you want yours to be absorbing and effective, it is good to have the strategy of striving to make the next better than the last.

These tips have survived the test of wide and thorough application:

- In the course of the webinar, don't start out by stridently announcing that there is something valuable to share but it won't be revealed until the end. Tactfully dole out the "tease" in bite-size chunks throughout the event with a view to being educational or informative and not commercial.
- In the same vein, don't let your strategy be to force attendees to stay for the entire event. If they have scheduled themselves to be there only for a segment of the agenda that applies to their situation, there is more to lose from the antagonism of making them wait until the end to get the information they need.
- Never read verbatim from the slide being presented; paraphrasing the text is more professional and convincing.
- For the sake of comprehension, keep the slide count to under 30 slides per hour or roughly one every two minutes.
- Context must be give-and-take by design to sustain the audience's interactive participation.
- Employing more than one speaker, preferably a combination of men and women, helps maintain audience interest.
- Be sure of your expertise with the technology to guarantee a smooth performance.

Live Events

The more traditional live events tend to uncover more sales-ready leads than webinars and are especially effective at later stages of the buying process. Often more seriously interested in the topic, attendees are willing to spend the necessary time away from the office. Live events by nature of the venue usually engage more of the attendees' senses, which research shows helps anchor and retain content longer.

The variety of locations for live presentations ranges from institutions of higher learning to hotels, resorts, restaurants, independent meeting facilities, and movie theaters. Live events typically require greater investment in meeting space, logistics, catering, and staff. A professional meeting planner/facilitator is invaluable the first time around.

Whether webinar or live event, take into account that the objective is to provide valuable information that buttresses learning and provides insights into the subject at hand. Give the audience something to sink its teeth into in the interest of expediency and time.

Archived Events

Good, interesting content is invariably forwarded by attendees to colleagues and others. Therefore, don't overlook the importance of archiving webinars or webcasts for postevent distribution to inquiring Web site visitors and others. You can also use these archived events for promotion in follow-up e-mail campaigns. Archived webinars have been known to pull in more virtual attendees than attendees of the original event. One of my clients registered only 85 attendees for a live webinar but 14 months later tracked over 1,500 archive attendees for the recorded version of the same event.

The concept is also effective for replaying or rebroadcasting live events. Digitally record the audio or video, edit the content, and burn it to CD or DVD for easy distribution. Digital files can be posted to your Web site for retrieval as downloadable audio on MP3s or streaming video.

Outsourcing Talent

So, you have a topic of substance that promises to revolutionize your company's image and it is important that the concept be professionally presented. There is, though, a certain lack of comfort in the company's capabilities for putting its best foot forward in an instance like this. Enter the outside presenter. Consider outsourcing the task and bringing in a professional speaker (or speakers) who lines up with your value proposition and adds the extra touch that will take you to the next level. Heightened interest, better presence, greater visibility, increased attendance, and improved cost-effectiveness are only a few of the latent benefits, and the ultimate payoff could be incalculable.

The goal is normally to position the company in context of thought leadership. As a result, look to someone in your industry who already represents that role and is recognized as an authority. The sources are many. Quite often, assuming you both are in the same field of interest, outsiders can be given incentive with the knowledge that your good database provides simultaneous opportunity for them to get in front of appropriate people at the right companies. There are even instances where the value proposition is so appealing that speakers are motivated to barter their services in lieu of cash or other considerations.

The process of outsourcing speaking talent usually focuses on:

- Finding someone who is a veteran of the specific type of event, e.g., webinars, or at least has a working knowledge of its techniques.
- Determining that the candidate speaks clearly and passionately with an air of believability and credibility.
- Providing the selectee with ample background information to ensure a knowledgeable and credible presentation.
- Minimizing biographical portrayal of the speaker, for purposes of maintaining interest, when introduced to attendees.
- Being selective in choosing presenters who use the language of and who are at the level of the attendees or can speak to it.
- Familiarizing everyone concerned with the technology that will be employed, i.e., phones, computers, etc.

Regardless of who does the presenting, insider or outsider, the content of the presentation must be right and proper. If it is, you shine. If it is not . . . Remember that you and/or your company are in the spotlight; do as you hope you will be judged.

Event marketing via webinars or any other technique is not unlike the underlying concept of lead generation; the end is only the beginning. Efforts do not conclude by immediately and improperly relaying the attendance information to sales for action.

Planning Your Event

As the event begins to take form and you have an idea of what you want it to be, take your plan framework and ask yourself where you think promotional emphasis should be put to push it over the top. Proceed by answering in detail:

- Have campaign objectives been defined?
- What is the target audience?
- What will attendees gain from this event?
- What is the topic and how is it best described?

- Does the topic tie to your value proposition?
- Is content appropriate and ready?
- What is the agenda?
  - Are presenters named and set?
  - Is there a design or theme?
  - Type of event?
  - Format?
  - Planned length?
- How will the success of the event be measured?
  - Impact of making plan?
  - How many contacts will be added to lead nurturing?
  - How many touch points will be reached?
  - Rate of sales-ready leads becoming bona fide prospects?
  - Who is responsible for collecting and handling the results?
- How will ROI be measured?
  - By qualified leads?
  - By attendance?
  - By cost per registrant?
  - By cost per attendee?
  - By cost per sales-ready lead?
- Is the event adequately budgeted?
  - Total expense?
  - How many attendees are planned?
  - Anticipated cost per attendee?

Once the plan has been established, the next step is to develop a strategy to promote the event.

Promotion Strategy

In form, a promotional strategy for hyping the event can be intimidating to contemplate. On the other hand, if extrapolated from the planning components, with a dash of logic, it is quite clear that promotion is vital to the success of the event. These tips may help in putting a promotion strategy together:

- Take a multimodal approach—send out e-mails, mailings, and phone key desired customers.
- Be especially careful in evaluating tactics.
- Design promotional materials to the style of the sales team.
- Enlist the sales team to send personal notes of invitation to leads being worked.

- Make registration procedures prominent and clear.
- Employ a well-thought-out e-mail template for confirming registration.
- Make event details a conspicuous element on your Web site.
- Gear up your database.
- Develop survey questions before, during, and after the event as deemed necessary.
- Use a pre-event survey that inquires about:
  - What the registrant is hoping to learn.
  - What attracted the registrant.
  - How the registrant heard about the event.
  - If there are colleagues that should be invited.
- Incorporate a reminder messages schedule (webinar).
  - Week prior—confirmation and instructions.
  - Day before.
  - Early day of.
  - Personal phone calls.

A multimodal approach is key, and Figure 11-1 shows various ways you can promote your event. Each element in your lead generation arsenal will serve a purpose in drawing qualified registrants and maximizing their attendance. PR can and should play an important role in promotion.

A carefully crafted e-mail campaign to prospects already opted into your lead nurturing program will get the ball rolling, as will a personal call inviting your teleprospecting contacts. An event is an excellent occasion to make a call. A special addition to the Web site for more information is also helpful, and the Web site provides a centralized method of registration and tracking. And

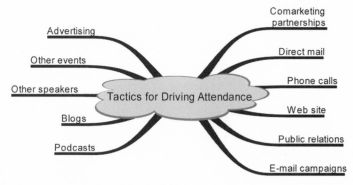

Figure 11-1 Event promotion tactics

a personalized direct mail piece, e-mail, or phone call can solidify the attendance of those already registered.

Execution

A source of continuing amazement is how often some will invest in putting an event together only to have it fail to deliver because promotion was inadequate, not only in terms of tactical attention, but also the time allocated to build interest in it. Few if any tactics guarantee success, particularly if utilized individually and alone, and it is not inappropriate to allow a three-to-six-month lead time for planning, development, and execution.

Practice may not necessarily make perfect, but it certainly helps. And frequency of events provides a greater comfort level that makes everything easier to accomplish. For any event, it's important to work ahead. To start, schedule a series of events over the space of a year, perhaps one event each quarter, depending on the strategic wisdom of that kind of timing or regularity. Once concept and development of an event are in motion, establish a pre-event time line that might look something like this plan for a webinar:

- **Six weeks prior:** Update Web site with event details, registration landing page, and home page access.
- **Five weeks prior:** Update signature files for sales team e-mail template, update blogs, alert any partners.
- **Four weeks prior:** Send direct mail invitations, launch PR campaign, and initiate news release online.
- **Three weeks prior:** Phone follow-up to direct mail, begin e-mail campaign.
- **Two weeks prior:** E-newsletter announcement of event.
- **One week prior:** Phone reminders to registrants and reminder e-mail.
- **One day prior:** Follow-up reminder e-mail.
- **Two hours prior:** Second reminder e-mail.

After the Event

Your odds of success in converting attendees to customers take a great leap forward with proper follow-up after the show—or after any comparable event, be it trade show, webinar, etc. Start with an immediate and openly sincere call or note of thanks and ask for response to a quick postevent survey that poses, with respect to what they perceived of you, such questions as:

Creative, high-quality content can dramatically build event attendance and assure credibility, positive word of mouth, and a buzz for future events. My company has increased webinar registrations by 255 percent with core content development and promotion tactics, and the last three events brought in 280, 495, and 995 registrants respectively. While average industry attendance runs about 30 percent of registrations, ours is 41 percent. We believe these successes are directly attributable to intensive and consistent observation of these tenets governing good event promotion.

- Did they like what they saw and heard?
- Is the information valuable?
- Are there suggestions for future events?

In addition to this schematic of postevent protocol and with the event completed, pay special heed to:

- Moving the registration and attendance date to your database for tracking.
- Sharing useful and relevant information.
  - Where feasible, e.g., webinars, creating a transcript of the entire presentation for attendees and for general distribution in the future.
  - Capturing questions asked and answers provided in a document for attendees.
  - Posting the entire event archive to include an offer for such adjuncts as pertinent articles or white papers.
- Compiling event metrics.
  - Number of registrants.
  - Number of attendees.
  - Number of no-show registrants.
  - Names of registrants.
  - Names of attendees.
  - Names of no-show registrants.
  - Percentage of attendees to registrants.
  - Cost per attendee.
  - Number of attendees converted to sales-ready leads.
  - Cost per sales-ready lead.
  - Percentage of sales-ready leads moved into the sales funnel as prospects.
  - Number of contacts added to lead nurturing database.

- Reviewing.
    - Surveying responses.
    - Things learned, things that worked, things that did not work.
    - Possible changes.
    - Sales team feedback.

If nothing else, do three things:

1. Immediately get in touch with those indicating that they want to be contacted.
2. Qualify attendees before sending their names to sales.
3. Contact the no-show registrants and offer to send the event content, invite them to future events, and agree to future contact.

Trade Shows

Applying some of the tactical principles to participation in trade shows can be difficult because the targeted end-result is not a complete reckoning of who was there and for what purpose. Even this is changing as organizers work to prescreen and track attendance better for the benefit of exhibitors. In any case, exhibiting at trade shows is another event tactic that doesn't stop when the show closes and the booth shuts down. And again, at the end, few if any of those who have shown interest in your product or service could be certified as sales-ready leads. To relay unqualified booth visitor inquiries to sales shoots them right into a black hole, likely never to be seen again. Julia O'Connor, the president of Trade Show Training says, "80 percent of leads [inquiries] are not followed up on after the show and the 20 percent who are contacted, can't all be handled the same way because they are in different places in the buying process."[1]

Instead—as you would potential leads of similar ilk from other kinds of events—input the names into the database, perform database hygiene, and complete any missing profile data required by the ideal customer profile. Then relay the names to the qualification team to be qualified as sales-ready opportunities for the sales team.

When names of registrants are available, as with seminars, it always works to further apply to premarket potential attendees with an invitation before the show to stop by your booth (perhaps adding an incentive of your choice).

1 Interview with Julia O'Connor, President, Trade Show Training, 5/5/2005.

"I'm Not Ready!"

It is important that the marketing department involves the sales force early in the process of shaping an event. This will aid the flow of constructive feedback and input from the front lines. Note, though, that after the event, it may be all too tempting for marketers to pass along a list of event attendees to sales

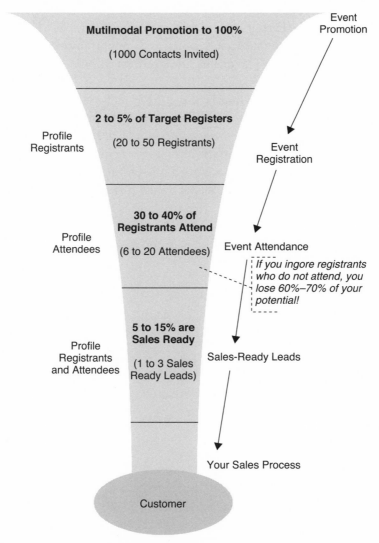

Figure 11-2 Lead generation funnel for events

before applying the qualification process as measured against the universal lead definition. Too many marketers have brought their developing lead generation undertakings to a grinding halt by rushing unprocessed and as a result unqualified event attendees right to the sales team. Don't do it. It can't be said too often that 9 times out of 10, event participants do not represent sales-ready leads.

The conversion rates illustrated in Figure 11-2 reflect industry research and my company's own research on event marketing programs for companies with a complex sale. Even if most attendees have an interest in what you have to say, it does not mean that each is a sales-ready opportunity. Where are they in their buying process? The qualification process still must be applied and conversation must develop.

Event marketing in its hugely varied form and utilizing the myriad of tools available to it is a vital and exciting aspect of operations for many businesses. For lead generation and the complex sale, although a "live" themed activity in the truest meaning of the term, event marketing narrows its focus to techniques that ensure a concentrated one-on-one interface with targeted audiences and indisputable high return on the investment.

Chapter Twelve

Lead Generation on the Web

Once upon a time there was a face-to-face meeting between a decision maker and a salesperson. As a matter of fact, once upon a time there were a lot of face-to-face meetings between decision makers and salespeople. Meetings like this were frequent and important because from them came the exchange of information and ideas that would be vital to buying decisions ultimately made by customers and potential customers alike. It was the way things were in the business-to-business world of the complex sale.

Then along came the Internet. Those once-valued meetings started taking place later in the buying process, if at all. Now, executive buyers, technical buyers, and corporate end-users found themselves with search engines at their fingertips. All they had to do was gain access to a wildly proliferating choice of new Web sites to find the specific information required in evaluating available products and services that would fill their needs. And with the Internet, they no longer had to wait to get the information from the sales-level individuals who serviced their business. Clearly the Internet has become the go-to resource for most companies looking for solutions. Today, in many instances, marketers are seizing control of the company Web site. With this comes the responsibility for optimizing its heralded potential to turn visitors into customers. Is your Web site ready to fill the role of presales consultant?

Forbes magazine asked companies what they consider to be their single most important source of business information. The responses were:

- 49 percent of C-Level executives said the Internet,
- 57 percent of large corporation senior management said the Internet,
- 85 percent of all respondents said they use search engines.[1]

1 "Day in the Life of C- Level Executives Part V," *Forbes*, September 2004.

Search Engine Optimization

Search engine optimization, the process of increasing the number of visitors to a Web site by ranking high in the results of search engines across the Internet, is essential for directing more traffic to a specific Web site. Some business-to-business marketers remain focused solely on enhancing the search marketing capabilities of their Web sites, i.e., indiscriminately generating more traffic at the expense of Web site content and relevance. This stems from the misconception that added traffic equals a greater number of inquiries and leads and, in due course, more sales. Search engine optimization assumes a lower rung in the climb towards more effective lead generation in the business-to-business sector.

The ever-changing nature of search engine optimization makes today's search practices obsolete tomorrow, and it seems quite apparent from a lead generation viewpoint that overemphasizing the role of search engine optimization and pay-per-click tactics can indeed have negative impact on visitor conversion and return on investment. Which is not to say search engine ranking isn't a major factor in the business-to-business sales cycle and should be minimized. Rather, as a tool, it must be used as circumstances dictate, with balance that lends greater credence to attracting the right kind of visitors. A more successful approach that many marketers and skilled PR professionals are employing is to use the press release in conjunction with their Web site. The press release generates better results from search engine optimization by choosing and loading key words that a targeted audience is known to be looking for.

The total number of visitors to a Web site is meaningless to the lead generation program—unless by some quirk all happen to be qualifiable sales leads, in part, the "right kind" of visitors. Without a lead generation strategy, efforts to bring traffic to the site for the sake of traffic do little to move the sales needle. A Web site that is oriented to the demands of a lead generation program attracts the kind of visitors that results in the capture of a lot of valuable inquiries. Three underlying Web site design principles should be looked to for facilitating this. Let's examine each of these.

Inform

The importance of using PR efforts to drive Web site visibility cannot be denied. People are attracted to Web sites for a variety of reasons, and it is to your advantage to promote yours as an easily accessed source of information appropriate to the needs of your potential customers. There is little point in having a Web site that no one visits.

Take an outsider's point of view in developing your approach; evaluate your Web site as you might if you were a potential customer and then tailor how you want to position it accordingly. When you browse through it, consider:

- What does it convey about the company?
- Is it professionally done?
- Does it have the right information?
- Is desired information quick and easy to locate?
- What value is perceived?
- What is the next step?

An attention-getting way to attract potentially interested parties to your Web site is to prominently offer a resource center, which might include recordings or reprints of various presentations, e.g., seminars, webinars, articles, case studies, and white papers. Another is to clearly call out an archive library of past events and indexed descriptions. With multimodal tactics, many of these resources likely have been created for other opportunities and are waiting to be offered on your Web site. Another informative feature—and one that inspires the confidence that you know what you are doing—is a list of companies you have done business with along with a few endorsements of existing customers who may have had something good to say about you.

By whatever other means, the Web site, while informative, must attract and clearly articulate your unique value proposition while conveying that it is one you would want to return to. It should be reflective of what and who your audience is and what you have determined the audience has greatest interest in. It must not be difficult to navigate, nor should it presume to make demands on the customer or potential customer's time or efforts to secure further content that could just as well be incorporated into the format or as a link.

Engage

Converting the Web site visitor to qualified lead status is a tall order, but the results can be dramatic due to the extraordinarily large visitor potential. In pursuit of increasing the ratio of visitors to qualified leads, it is beneficial to examine:

- What is happening on each page to hold your visitor's interest.
- What actions you want your visitor to take.
- What appeals to that person or typically to the role of that person.
- What the visitor needs to do for more information or to make contact.
- What you could be doing better.

Many visitors will most likely be in the early stages of their buying processes. They are still gathering background information while refining their short lists of companies deserving further attention. Other company principals may be involved as well. Although not visible at this point, they could very well appear later as important touch points, represented by influencers and decision makers whose roles are yet to become evident. Nevertheless, the visitor, though perhaps doing only initial research that will eventually be handed off to another individual, is your concern at the moment and must be viewed as the contact to be developed.

The visit of a higher-up executive decision maker often indicates that the prospective company is further along in its buying process. These individuals may have the research and opinions of the "pathfinder" and are ready to make their own conclusions. C-level decision makers gravitate to your "about us" page for information about management, company history, strengths, and anything else that might give them a better picture of whether you would understand their needs. They usually are concerned about "fit." Executive decision makers admit to putting a lot of stock in companies well ranked on search engines because it indicates to them that what you say is relevant to their needs. When requiring more information, their inquiries likely will come in the form of a phone call.

Some companies incorporate a thank-you page that, along with requesting the typical confirmation information, offers such incentives as resource materials, e.g., brochures, catalogs, etc. Regardless of who or from what level, however, when someone has taken the time to fill out your Web site form asking for information, consider it a wonderful start for developing a relationship and respond to it accordingly.

Convert

Turning visitors into high-quality leads is regularly a matter of how quickly you respond to their inquiries. Though they obviously are entitled to your answer with all due haste, research indicates that nearly half of all inquiries are not followed up within two weeks—if at all.

How can that be, you ask? Sad but true, all else being equal, many of the issues of proper follow-up have to do with a lead generation program that is all or in part on the wrong track, incomplete, or simply not taken seriously. There may not be a good connection between the Web site and the database. The sales team may not be in tune with what constitutes a good inquiry and is too busy wasting time chasing poor-quality leads. The Web site's request for information may not be providing the necessary data to determine the value of the inquiry.

The shoulds and should-nots bear repeating time and again:

- The sales team should not be put in the unfortunate position of receiving Web inquiries (or any others) directly and unqualified.
- The Web site contact form should be concise and to the point for maximum response and to populate the database for the sales team's benefit.
- Inquiries should be researched thoroughly with online database tools like HillSearch, Dun & Bradstreet, or InfoUSA and appended with any other information required to round out the ideal customer profile.
- There should be the mind-set that each and every bona fide inquiry deserves an immediate show of interest on your part.
- The process of relaying sales-ready leads that have passed the universal lead definition test to the sales team for follow-up should be speeded up.
- Contact should be established with potential customers that are not yet sales ready but are primed to opt into the lead-nurturing program.
- All inquiries should be responded to with a prompt note of thanks for the interest and for taking time to inquire, regardless of whether the inquiring party fits the ideal customer profile.
- A supplementary e-mail thank-you should be used to share added relevant data.
- There should be a balance between collecting information and providing value, i.e., be careful about requiring registration to receive anything worthwhile.

Strategic relations consultant Justin Hitt recommends that marketers balance unencumbered free information with information that requires registration. "While I'll give some information free," he says, "I recommend to my clients they collect enough information to deliver [the] white paper and follow up with other offers that further qualify the prospect. My lead generation

> A company generating 12,000 leads a year centrally via Web site quali-
> fies all of its leads against the universal lead definition. The standard is
> to distribute leads to sales immediately upon qualifying them. By edict,
> the inside sales team then calls the leads within 15 minutes to an hour
> after receiving them. A meeting with a salesperson is subsequently
> scheduled. Should it be determined that a lead went more than 24 hours
> without being followed up on, the salesperson responsible can expect a
> call from management. If more than 48 hours, the salesperson risks
> much more.
>
> Tough duty? You bet, but it works. A lead conversion rate that effec-
> tively triples the industry's and a rapidly growing rate of sales are the proof.

landing pages pull 17 percent to 23 percent, but I only ask for a first name
and e-mail name and address for physical items. If someone is interested
enough in requesting more information, then it's my responsibility to stay in
touch. My follow-up then works on understanding their unique situation,
time frame to purchase, and ability to buy."

At the beginning, alacrity of follow-up is often the best indication that
your company is a disciplined leader in its field and is enthused about doing
business.

Beyond practicing fast and eager follow-up, the goal of directly increasing the number of Web-site-generated inquiries is considerably enhanced by
paying careful attention to Web site landing pages and "contact us" forms.
Both are very good initial steps in developing the image that you are an
expert at what you do.

What Is a Landing Page?

Your Web site serves two primary functions: discovering current interests and
providing information relevant to those interests. Attracting Web site visitors
is the easy part. Converting them to qualified leads is more difficult, and
from the standpoint of lead generation, conversion is the purpose of the
landing page.

Every page on your Web site is potentially a landing page. A landing page
is the place the visitor has reached upon clicking a hyperlink. The link could
have been from any number of sources: search engines, e-mail, a pay-per-
click (PPC) ad, or another Web site. If coming from a search engine, a great

many visitors are clicking deep into your Web site and not directly to your home page.

It is important, therefore, to design each and every page to clearly direct the visitors—your potential customers—to actions you want them to take, no matter where in your site they make contact. Properly designed landing pages alleviate your home page from doing all the heavy lifting. If you use pay-per-click advertising on your Web site, it is wise to drive potential customers to ad-specific landing pages and not to your home page. When properly set up, a sponsored ad reveals a current interest, which is valuable information that should not be jeopardized by linking to an irrelevant or generalized page. And once more, the objective is to make it easy to find the information being sought.

If you ask that a form be completed, keep the form short and the process simple. Don't create unnecessary complications. Alternative means of reaching you should be offered for those who don't like to fill out forms, e.g., phone number, fax number, e-mail address. You can gather detailed information later as the prospect moves through the sales cycle.

Experienced marketers test different versions of landing pages, carefully evaluating the efficacy of such elements as headlines, copy length, calls-to-action, and format, always with a view towards measuring and improving conversion rates. They also give extensive attention to:

- What they want their visitors to do.
- A clear call to action that provides all the required information and direction for visitors to move forward.
- Removing or reducing unnecessary elements that distract or make the page less focused on anticipated interests and desired results.
- Good, proven page layout that follows prescribed attention-getting design and ensures easy reading.
- Consistency of design and presentation.
- Relevance to what prospects with knowledge of the company's business likely would be searching for.

According to Anne Holland, publisher of MarketingSherpa, 50 percent of Web visitors spend just eight seconds scanning a company's Web site landing page before deciding to leave.[2] She also points out that marketers who

---

2 Anne Holland, "Landing Page Handbook: How to Raise Conversions—Data & Design Guidelines," MarketingSherpa, February 2005.

regularly test and tweak their landing pages realize a 40 percent increase in Web site conversions.[3] Enough said?

Tracking Web Site Return on Investment

In the task of converting inquiries to leads and ultimately in determining return on investment, your Web site log files are an important tool for measuring to what extent search engine optimization is a cost-effective factor. By pinpointing where traffic originates and the accompanying click-stream, you have the means of tracking the path visitors are taking to your site. Log files can be tied into the database to view how often a visitor clicked on and the attendant click stream (pages visited and in what order).

To track Web site return on investment in terms of lead generation, you must go beyond the data collected on the Web site log files. Basic metrics such as number of clicks, unique visitors, number of opt-in e-mails gathered, and number of inquiries (forms) filled out are simply not enough to determine your actual ROI.

Mal Watlington writing in WebProNews has noted; "In the business-to-business world, customer behavior and the length of the buying cycle make the connection between on-the-web activity and the decision to purchase much more difficult to trace."[4]

Tracking return on investment is daunting but not impossible. In the business-to-business complex sale, most of the selling is off line. The sales process is actually a long series of microconversions resulting from ongoing dialogue. The key is to tie the off-line activities together with the on-line. With the focus on tracking metrics and microconversions that go beyond the lead, both on-line and off-line, it is easy to see that multimodal-based lead generation with all of its touch points is best coordinated and managed through the database. The database can be used to report those touch points that resulted in new business and identify the role played by the Web site in lead conversion.

Metrics required for Web site tracking and arriving at conclusions about return on investment commonly are associated with:

3 Interview with Anne Holland, President, MarketingSherpa Inc., 11/08/2004.
<http://blog.startwithalead.com/weblog/podcast/index.html>
4 Mal Watlington, "Getting The 'R' In ROI From Web-Generated Leads," WebProNews, 29 November 2004, HYPERLINK "http://www.webpronews.com/ebusiness/ebusinesstactics/wpn-8-20041129Getting theRinROIfromWebGeneratedLeads.html"

- Inquiries.
- Visitor-to-inquiry conversion rate.
- Visits to "contact us" pages.
- Inbound phone calls from Web site 800 number.
- White paper requests.
- Newsletter registrations.
- Opt-in e-mail addresses.
- Key words clicked on most frequently.
- Key words producing the best inquiries.
- Key words producing the worst inquiries.

Bring it all Together

So, you have built a Web site that can engage, inform, and convert potential customers. You have designed to bring in the right type of visitor. It is relevant to your target audience, has thought-leading content, and is firmly rooted in your unique value proposition. As a destination, it is a place people visit for the insights and information they are searching for. It depends on a centralized database and is ready to track activity. What do you do now to alert possible visitors that you offer the best potential for their success?

Enabling the Web site to be viewed favorably by the major search engines, search engine optimization is a huge factor in getting the right visitors. A great many Web site operators pay homage to the importance of key words—search terms—but do little to facilitate their crucial role in ensuring a favorable position in search rankings, search engine optimization.

Whether automated methods—search engine "spiders"—or manual implementation are used to facilitate this, the greater the number of appropriate key words in the site, the better the indexing and the higher the search ranking. Key words basically make the search engine what it is. Complicated tricks that attempt to fool search engines with imbedded HTML code and tags are largely ineffective. And pay-per-click campaigns—ads on search engines for specific searches with a fee for each click on the ad—are time-consuming and frequently more costly than they are worth from the standpoint of the complex sale.

Currently, two primary elements reliably drive favorable search engine indexing and ranking. They are cross-linking and search term relevance.

Cross-linking is the practice of adding to your Web site a link to another Web site or a link on another Web site to yours—with the consent of the other Web site, of course. It is a referral process of sorts. The objective is to bring other related resources to the attention of the visitor in an effort to make your site more content-rich. Search engines may consider Web sites with contextual cross-links to be more relevant and as a result rank them higher for a given search term. Cross-links can also generate more traffic from the referring site.

The second element is search term relevance, which works in concert with cross-linking. Conducting a search on a major search engine often brings an immeasurable number of results, but many of these are valueless in their significance. Search engines typically return the results of a user's query in order of "relevance score." The more relevant that the search engine identifies the Web page or Web site to be, the higher it will rank it. Relevancy is determined by both the uniqueness of the search term, contextual cross-links, and something called search term density. Search term density is the number of key words on a page, and if key words are used often in context, the search engine may conclude that your site is most relevant. A greater measure of relevant results can be expected when the search term is narrowly specific or unique.

If your site clearly articulates a unique value proposition and provides targeted and relevant content aligned with that value proposition, the target audience should have little trouble finding you when looking for what you have to offer.

Volumes could be written on using the Web to accomplish better lead generation, but the principles can be summed up as follows:

- It is important to focus on relevance and visitor conversion first when seeking greater search engine optimization.
- Your value proposition should relate to the search terms your prospects will logically use.
- It is important to have keyword density that accurately reflects the value proposition.
- Your Web site should be perceived as having high-value, thought-leading content.
- Resources—collateral materials—should be provided freely with little or no qualification.
- For continuity and efficiency's sake, it is good to use content created for other lead generation activities.
- Inquiries must be responded to in a timely and professional manner.
- The easier for visitors to get information or contact you, the more likely dialogue will be opened.

- There should be multiple means of finding and reaching your Web site without difficulty.
- Your Web site should be integrated with your database for searching, scheduling, and record-keeping purposes.

The corporate Web site has been described as the fulcrum of today's lead generation activities. It is a highly effective method of delivering genuinely interested visitors that frequently translate into meaningful, new, qualified customer prospects.

Chapter Thirteen

Lead Generation and Direct Mail

Direct mail, by purest definition, is a form of marketing communication designed to reach targeted groups of potential customers by regular mail with the objective of generating awareness or action. A lot of good and enlightening information exists that discusses the value of direct mail in the marketing of products and services in general. Unfortunately, there isn't a lot of material focusing on its application as a lead generation tactic specifically for the complex sale. For companies that sell consumer products (or have a more transactional sale) direct mail is repeatedly a winning tactic. But when it comes to the complex sale, not only is direct mail ineffective by itself, but it is also frequently used incorrectly and even abused.

At first glance, it appears that many award-winning, integrated marketing campaigns relying heavily on direct mail have been celebrated as successful producers of sales leads. If you dig deeper, however, you will discover that most of the so-called "leads" in such cases are merely inquiries, and few if any are developed to yield the results expected in the complex sale setting.

In the final analysis, direct mail *as a medium entirely onto itself* is largely inappropriate for reaching executive-level decision makers and the multiple individuals who are involved in the buying process. Conversely, when the target is narrowly defined and the strategy is specifically geared to incorporating a follow-up function or supporting an existing dialog, direct mail becomes an important component of the entire lead generation strategy. Once more, it is the multimodal approach that enhances the potential in the process of generating leads.

Because it performs so well in other arenas, many marketing practitioners believe that direct mail will do the same for lead generation programs. In reality, direct mail is often expected to do more than it is capable of. Most direct mail, as we know, is a one-way transmission of information, and this is really the downside to its practicality in lead generation. A response mechanism like a postage-paid, self-addressed envelope or Web site URL can be added to hopefully elicit a reply, but there is still no assurance of making contact with the audience you want to reach if the direct mail piece stands alone.

With that in mind, let's look at how direct mail can be integrated into a lead generation campaign in a way that greatly improves its chance of becoming an effective hand-in-hand partner.

Targeted Campaigns

The first step in using direct mail in lead generation is to identify and define the target audience: the group of prospects to which the campaign has been designed to appeal. When not targeted, the campaign is mostly a matter of crossing your fingers and hoping the law of averages works in your favor. This is hardly an optimal strategy for guaranteeing leads that might bring about the complex sale.

For direct mail to be a productive component of your lead generation toolbox, your database to be used in managing the direct mail campaign must be leading-edge and totally up-to-date as described in context of other lead generation objectives I have covered. Outdated, unqualified, incomplete databases just won't cut it. Also, companies too often hire direct mail specialty firms for complex sale direct mail campaigns, and these firms don't take the role of the database seriously enough. Simply having a good list, from any standpoint, does little more than maintain status quo, if that.

Once you have verified that you're ready to do a direct mail program, give careful thought to the big picture of preparedness represented by:

- What you are trying to accomplish.
- Your value proposition and its relevancy.

A client chose to ignore the importance of telephone verification. A list acquired from a well-known data provider was to be the basis of an expensive mailing to top executives. Many of the next-day shipments—letter, brochure, and expensive umbrella with logo—ended up being directed to people who were retired, deceased, or otherwise no longer with the company. And to some who never worked for the company. So much for blind trust—and efficiency, effectiveness, and credibility.

- Who you are trying to reach.
- The language of the potential customer.
- Whether the potential customer knows "what's in it for me."
- Your direct mail message and how well it connects with your strategy.
- The database.
- Cleaning the database by:
  - Standardizing data (data normalization).
  - Removing erroneous data.
  - Removing duplicates.
  - Updating company information.
- Calling to verify contact information.
- Adding key contacts to the database.
- Reviewing results of last contact (if there was one).
- Calling for permission to send the mailing.
- Sending the mailing only to verified database contacts.
- Making the direct mail effort interactive with a follow-up call.
- Sending only direct mailings that the lead generation team has time to promptly follow up.

The basic rule in pursuing the qualifiable lead with direct mail is best illustrated by the tactic of book-ending a mailing by telephoning. First, call every contact on your list to inform them, directly or via voicemail message, that a direct mail campaign is about to get underway. Then call again to follow up once the mailing has been made. Perhaps it is a bit oversimplified, but this is a proven strategic approach reflecting the kind of multimodal activity that yields results and eliminates the appearance of just another directionless direct mailing left to its own devices.

Direct Mail for Follow-Up

For lead generation and the complex sale, follow-up is primarily where direct mail shines. In the lead-nurturing process, by extension, direct mail as a regularly utilized marketing component provides equally good results. This is especially true in lead nurturing when direct mail fulfills the objective of maintaining dialogue. You should consider its inherent ability to increase the effectiveness of other tactics whenever follow-up is important to realizing lead generation objectives. By whatever consideration, as a medium that is semi-intrusive at worst, direct mail is suitably cast in the role of ameliorating the intrusiveness attributed to the telephone call.

A firm selling to senior executives at Fortune 500 companies follows hard-and-fast rules in a very simple format when it engages direct mail to generate sales interest. Promoting a roundtable event, for example, starts with a phone call to the targeted recipient's assistant to verify correct information for sending the executive an invitation to an executive roundtable gathering. E-mail can be used as an alternative to the phone call. Then a handwritten invitation is mailed requesting the individual's presence at a peer company for an exclusive executive-only discussion and exchange of views hosted by a senior executive of the inviting company. The focus, usually a hot business topic, is moderated by the host firm. A follow-up call a day or two later, when it is reasonable to assume that the invitation has been received, makes for a tidy, results-oriented package that renders a high response rate.

The Pieces

The workhouse of business-to-business direct mail is still the one-page personalized letter sent in a #10 envelope. Kind of old-fashioned and probably not very creative in today's scheme of such things, but well-chosen words in short letter form can perform wonders when properly slotted in the campaign. Many marketers adhere to the traditional practice of employing the handwritten note to distinguish their message from all the others in this contemporary world of inkjet and laser-printed text and images. When sent by way of a hand-addressed envelope and postage stamp, the response rates from this mode are often off the scale. A note from one business-to-business CEO to another is good to consider under any circumstances.

Is something old new again? In recent years an interesting development bodes well for direct mail. With the proliferation of e-mail and its resulting abuses, direct mail has become almost a novel approach by comparison. Even though direct mail may not be as flexible, immediate, or economical as e-mail, if done with a high level of personalization and targeted to the appropriate players, it becomes almost an unexpected form of communication that affords another meaningful way to engage prospects.

Figure 13-1 includes other direct mail possibilities, and it should be obvious that any such available resources can serve to confirm and remind as dialogue progresses.

Multimodal marketing provides all manner of opportunities to involve direct mail as a tactic. A day after a direct mailing has been made, for

Figure 13-1 Direct mail possibilities

instance, it is prudent to call the recipients to alert them of their imminent arrival. Or you can integrate the direct mailing with the corporate Web site by including, with the mailing, a personalized URL that contains the recipient's name. With that URL and a code provided, the recipients get a distinctive Web landing page with information that is appropriate to their industries, companies, and job functions.

Too Creative?

Given that the real goal of lead generation is to help the sales team sell, the more elaborate the direct mail package, the better chance the selling effort has to be successful. Right? Not necessarily. Even though the prospect may display clear initiative and meet all of the definitions of a sales-ready lead, if the concept doesn't connect the value proposition with audience need, backlash may instead be the end result.

A rather stunning case in point: A company engaged in commercial leasing and counting 80 percent of Fortune 1000 companies as its customers sells in large part to senior executives. Wouldn't it be great to create an end-all direct mail campaign that would knock the socks off these executives, one that would deliver unprecedented new sales leads and, in turn, revenues? The upshot was a package composed of two baseballs bearing the signatures of all-time baseball greats Mickey Mantle and Willie Mays along with three display pedestals. A third baseball, with Hank Aaron's signature, was promised if a meeting was scheduled. The campaign was a hit if there ever was one. It generated spectacular excitement and a lot of appointments—but little in the way of new customers or increased revenue. Most CEOs wanted the third baseball so much that they missed the essence of the offer, the chance to learn if the company could meet their needs and improve their business.

Expensive premiums like this, sometimes referred to as appointment bribery, often pay scarce heed to the lead generation criteria and tend to mask the business objectives that were hoped to be accomplished. When the gift is gone, so is the opportunity.

When applied in proper perspective, direct mail is an effective tool for advancing the complex sale. As a one-to-one communication medium, it provides a way to introduce and sustain information to a very targeted audience—and, if need be, to nurture the audience over the course of the sales process. Timing is usually the key to the sale. The prospect may not have an immediate need for your product or service, but through an effective lead nurturing program using direct mail, you and your story can remain top of mind until the need does arise.

In considering direct mail, as with any tactic, it is important to understand the needs and wants of the target audience. Set measurable, attainable program objectives with calls to action that are relevant to the audience, and make sure that the medium is in the appropriate context. And in context of what? Follow-up, follow-up, follow-up.

Chapter Fourteen

Lead Generation and Referrals

For many companies over the past few decades, getting new business has depended on referrals and word-of-mouth recommendation, everything else aside. Now, however, the level of sophistication has changed; the bar has been raised.

Before we look at the ways changes have occurred, let's distinguish between referral and reference. Referral is the recommendation that a company or person makes on behalf of another, to a company seeking similar products or services. Referrals are deliberate, and referrals are eventually reciprocal; what goes around comes around. A reference, on the other hand, is a statement or testimony as to another's character or ability or value. References come from credible sources.

My wife's grandfather used to love to compare growing up in small-town Minnesota with modern-day living, the simple life before everything became complex and multitasked. Competing wasn't an essential way of life for most people. Everyone knew everyone else in town, and all coexisted with relative equanimity. Everyone knew their strengths and weaknesses, and all depended on one another in maintaining the integrity of their community.

The baker baked, the farmer farmed, the doctor doctored. No one knew about vertical integration or diversification, at least not by name or practical awareness, and "networking" was something everyone did but instead called it "staying in touch." Word-of-mouth was the glue that held it together. Technology has made word-of-mouth something very different in this twenty-first century.

Today, in the rapid and repeated expansion of choices that comes from—and results in—competition, getting noticed is frequently a big order that is largely driven by reputation. You don't build your own reputation; you have to earn it by delivering the best products or services and relying on others to help grow it by referring you to others. And those that do it most ably are your current customers, the ones who know and respect you for what you have done for them. They are often your best marketing tools.

Just what is your current customers' perception of you? The customers whose revenue pays the bills are the reason you are in business, and if you don't know, respect, and support those ongoing relationships and their reason for being, there is little more that can help you attain the kind of reputation you should be looking for.

A new CEO recently asked each member of his executive team to jot down a list of the company's top 10 customers, those that accounted for better than half of the firm's $300 million in sales. Only four knew the names of five of the customers, and the sales vice president struggled to name eight. "Whoa," the new CEO realized, "we need to do some work here. Like refocusing on the customer." He proceeded to put muscle in an internal Customer First initiative that ultimately yielded an attributable 115 percent increase in sales from existing customers. And to the point at hand—of growing future business with new customer relationships—customer referrals grew by over 100 percent.

When did you last take a personal interest in your customers and how you might better serve their wants and needs? A "How're you doing?" now and then can work wonders, and turnabout is fair play.

I wonder if serving a great variety of clients involved in the complex sale sometimes brings me too close to the problem to see the solution, but I am increasingly convinced that generating new business hinges on referrals more than anything else.

Recently, Frederick F. Reichheld, author of *The Loyalty Effect: The Hidden Force Behind Growth, Profits, and Lasting Value* and recognized expert in loyalty, seemed to substantiate that notion when he asked in the *Harvard Business Review*, "Would you recommend our products or services to a business peer?"[1] Two years of research confirmed that customers' enthusiastic referral of companies directly correlated with the companies' growth rate. When customers act as references, they do more than indicate that they have received good economic value from the company; they put their own reputations on the line. If you are not asking this of your customers—and getting the right answer—you could be generating word-of-mouth all right, but not the kind you are looking for.

Therefore, when customers can easily and in good conscience speak to your upstanding reputation by referral, you have to be pretty certain that you consistently provide them with significant value and have developed equity

1 Frederick F. Reichheld, "The One Number You Need to Grow," *Harvard Business Review*, 1 Dec. 2003,

in the relationship. The complex sale demands their enthusiastic word-of-mouth endorsement when it comes time to refer you to a potential new customer. This is in effect an untapped resource.

Just because an existing customer purchased from you does not mean the customer should be ignored after the sale. Corporate apathy has an unfortunate way of entering the equation, and the sales and marketing mentality must be jogged by checks that will preclude this. Does anyone care? Yes, and so will you.

There is a popular poster with a phone entangled in cobwebs on a dusty desk and admonishing not to take care of the customers so they'll leave us alone. It is sad commentary on the too-frequent propensity to be apathetic.

On the reverse side of the coin, therefore, the importance of your experience with current customers in developing a value proposition comes to the fore again when it is time to work on earning a good reputation. Why not add these questions when you talk with your customers?

- Would you refer our company to others if the opportunity presented itself?
- Would you agree to act as a reference if requested?
- If not, what can we do to earn your trust?

Also, while you are at it, seek their permission to cite their endorsement of your products or services where appropriate in your marketing communications materials, and on your Web site. And give serious consideration to adding the very same existing customers to your lead nurturing program as a means of engendering new business.

As your company increasingly assumes the role of thought leader, you may find that you receive referrals from companies that you have never done business with. That is when reputation has certifiably kicked in, when all that work earning an outstanding reputation starts to pay off.

In its quest for results like that, a leading knowledge management company used information gathered in its lead generation program to add new partners and improve the relationship with existing partners in complementing businesses. The focus was product-driven companies with revenues of $500 million to $2 billion. It was determined that many of these customers had existing relationships with consulting firms that would assist with vendor selection and implementation. The goal was to develop partnerships with the consulting firms to provide ongoing support after the solutions were implemented.

From this came the strategy of verifying correct contact information and requesting opt-ins for their lead nurturing activities. If it was determined that some were further along in the process and information was complete and showing an active initiative that fit the established universal lead definition, they were relayed as sales-ready to the direct sales team. In most cases, however, it was vitally important to learn the names of the respective consulting firms so they could be added to the operating database and categorized by description of size as small, medium, or large. All represented potential non-competitive partners with a common customer focus.

Able to approach each on the strength of specific clients previously contacted and interested in what the partnership opportunity might offer them, the CEO then began CEO-level conversations with the largest firms, the vice president of sales with the medium-size firms, and the sales team with the smallest, all in pursuit of developing partnerships with the consulting firm prospects.

The program was very successful. The CEO confided that each consulting firm referral was equivalent to an extra salesperson. It worked because the consulting firms were carefully approached knowledgably and confidently with respect to relationships with their clients. The callers were able to position themselves as trusted advisors, and the new partnerships proved to be genuinely productive collaborations of effort.

Expert Referrals

To develop referrals from experts that will generate more sales leads entails positioning yourself for a better understanding of the experts' points of view, which will in turn paint a better picture of courses of action to take in the future. It is important to identify your industry's key players and opinion shapers with a view towards getting to know who they are and what they stand for. Your research should include learning whether they are affiliated with companies that fit your ideal customer profile. If they are, you might find it constructive to attempt to get to know more of your customers' trusted advisors by making a first call to introduce yourself as someone with a mutual interest, which of course would be the same customer.

It probably goes without saying, but efforts to strike up acquaintances with the experts should always be presaged by complimentary interest in them and how they became what they are. Once you have their confidence, you stand a very good chance of being received into the ranks of resources that could be of help to their customers. And don't forget, they may bank on you as a potential referral for them as well.

These experts can also become your source of speakers and other event presenters. Or you may want to comarket an event and share the attendees

It has long been documented that staying in possession of and marketing to existing customers costs one-fifth that of developing new customer relationships. A client was trying to generate additional business with a Fortune 500 company with 19 divisions. There was visibility into six of the divisions, and three were already customers. The buying decision process was decentralized with the exception of a few loose integration rules, and each division was autonomous in its dealings with vendors.

An executive briefing program was developed to invite the targeted divisions to hear mini-case studies of other, interdivisional company projects currently underway that might be pertinent to what they were doing. Insights and communication from the three customer/divisions were instrumental in conducting these sessions and the company's presence in the three divisions no doubt gave added credibility to the effort. Now visible in 15 of the 19 divisions, the client has expanded internal touch points from 25 contacts to 45. And two $1 million pilot programs recently got started as a result. Internal referral at its best.

list. Also, there is often opportunity, simply for the asking, to post articles and materials of their creation on your Web site or as links. The ultimate objective is to get some of that credibility to rub off on you.

Internal Touch Points

By their nature or because that is just what they are expected to do, some salespeople are quite adept at building referral relationships, although there may be no financial incentive to do so. While this may be true sporadically, what gets paid gets done more, and referral selling, as a result, should be included in the compensation plan for maximum productivity. With referrals a part of the sales team's financial incentive, the salesperson is going to give this aspect of increasing sales output much more attention.

A properly constructed lead generation program has the built-in flexibility for assessing and developing revised, stronger customer relationships in accordance with demands placed on it by change in situation, place, or time.

Referrals and word-of-mouth are increasing the odds of success for many businesses across a wide scope of industries and are key to creating more and better sales leads in the complex sale.

Another good referral scenario occurred when a large employee financial service provider retained my firm to gain additional market share with large employers who already had well-entrenched relationships with the client's competitors through brokerages recommending the competitors' products. The products were essentially commoditized, but because of the multimillion dollar size of a sale, the sales process was regarded as complex.

Initial strategies were to attempt to directly influence the brokers to acquire our client's solutions. There was little success, however. The brokerages had no interest in adding further products to their already bursting portfolios.

As a result, the client company regrouped and embarked instead on placing its solutions directly with the brokerage customers, the large employers. An early phone lead generation program revealed that most if not all of these potential customers preferred to keep their business with the brokerages they were using. Undaunted, our client got permission from the end-use corporations to contact the brokerages in their behalf, hoping that that relationship would encourage evaluation of what it had to offer.

A new lead generation effort included a database that would ensure the relevancy of the calls. The calls were now to the brokerages and underwritten with a value proposition that was applicable to the revised circumstances, e.g., "I spoke to your customer, (_____), who was interested in our solution and gave me permission to contact *you* to review it so *you* could tell them more about it." The revised lead generation program today is very successful on the strength of a referral program structured to a unique challenge.

Chapter Fifteen

Blogs, Podcasting, and the Brave New World of Lead Generation

Since the very first moment I realized that my future would be consulting on complex sales issues to top-level executives, a very salient bit of advice has stayed with me: "Just be people with people." It is an exhortation that I frequently say to myself as a reminder to be real, straightforward, and sensitive in dealing with customers. And this mind-set is the essence of blogging, another new product of technology for promoting lead generation. Blogging has become a surprisingly effective tool for creating and perpetuating the image of companies and individuals as thought leaders and for reaching potential customers.

A blog is a body of information that is instantly published to a Web site. Short for weblog, the blog began and to a great extent still exists as a personal journal that frequently includes philosophical reflections, opinions, and discussions of specific issues along with a log of the author's favorite Web links. Blogs are usually presented in journal style and often include new material every day. Certain blogs have gained a wide following.

Blogs are new, hip, and everyone wants one. Blogs have zoomed to many millions in just a few years, and the promise of continued exponential growth seems mandated. So does their very diverseness. And their degree of excellence. As so often happens with something that catches on so quickly, blogs as a whole have a way to go before their collective level of quality can be described as keeping pace with their proliferation.

Blogs with specific focus on sales and marketing are increasingly common and today reach thousands of readers compared to virtually none a few years ago. Corporate blog users are far and away the smaller firms. The essential properties and characteristics of the corporate blog? First, the information it provides is devoid of the double-talk that symbolically or otherwise masks the true personality of the company and those who run it. And so for those firms acutely concerned about protecting their brand image—and most are—the essential truth portrayed in a blog may create a little confusion about what they really stand for. Listening, reflecting, and talking forthrightly are instead the rule, and if such qualities are not reflective of where a company wants to be, then likely the blog by virtue of strict definition is not in that company's best interests.

"Blogs," according to David Schatsky, chief of research of JupiterMedia Corporation's Jupiter Research unit, "are stirring sales leads from clients who otherwise might not have contacted us." Schatsky enthuses that scores of potential clients have contacted Jupiter in response to blogs.[1]

Blogging, the Great Equalizer

Experts estimate that as few as 7 percent of Fortune 500 companies have their own external blogs. Others say that could be closer to 10-20 percent. In either case, it is obvious that quite a number of companies are not active bloggers. Many larger companies who must contend with a much higher level of scrutiny—the Sarbanes-Oxley Act, SEC disclosures, the FTC, et al.—may have no interest in managing yet another risk, such as a blog. Also, there is that discomforting sense of needing to protect the company at every turn that leaves little room for the conventional lack of ambiguity in blogs.

So for now, blogs are not popular with the Fortune 500 crowd. Which means only that these larger organizations don't have their own; no doubt they spend a great deal of time keeping up with blogs of others in the same industry. As larger companies join the blogosphere, and there is no reason to think they won't as the medium becomes more sophisticated, they will have figured out how to balance perceived risk with the value of communication that is free from ambiguity. It is like the circus performer delicately balancing on the high wire—but still with the need for a safety net.

Smaller companies that are not as constrained by formality, hierarchy, or scrutiny have a distinct competitive advantage when it comes to blogs. Their compact size allows them the nimbleness to run circles around the big guys in certain settings. "While any size company can use such a strategy," the *Wall Street Journal*'s Riva Richmond writes, "small businesses may benefit most. Blogs offer little-known small businesses the name recognition and the chance to boost traffic well beyond what they would get if they were simply offering goods and services for sale."[2]

1 Doug Tsuruoka, "Blogs Bring a Boost to Jupiter Research," *Investors Business Daily*, 2 November 2004.
2 Riva Richmond, "Blogs Keep Internet Customers Coming Back," Wall Street Journal Online, March 2005. Copyright 2005 by Dow Jones & Co Inc, Reproduced with permission via Copyright Clearance Center.

Blogging is a strategic imperative in lead development for my company, the role played for our clients notwithstanding, because it is used in a variety of ways and means to support the sales process. The sales team regularly refers prospective clients to the company blog for demonstration of the expertise and relevance that have been touted. Blogging is also important to our lead nurturing program.

Search engines like blogs. When you are dealing within a narrow area of interest, blogs come up high in a search because of the sharp focus, keyword density, and cross-linking capabilities that facilitate rapid movement within search engines. Its relevancy gives my company's "B2B Lead Generation Blog" the enviable position of being at or near the top of Google's nearly endless list of "lead generation" Web sites.

Are You Ready to Blog?

Temper your enthusiasm about becoming a gung-ho blogger by evaluating, with all of the ramifications you can possibly think of, how you will use your blog. Start with:

- Why you think you should be blogging.
- What your writing would be about.
- The audience you would hope to attract.
- Your willingness to take the extra time required to cultivate relationships.

Once these issues are safely resolved and you have reached a reasonable level of comfort, the rest is a little easier. Blogging simply involves focusing on a subject in which you have an interest or expertise and are deeply passionate about, and the words will follow.

Many resources exist to help develop your blog knowledge, even blogs on the subject of blogging. Blogging would ordinarily be regarded by marketing people as a pull tactic, but when subscribed to via RSS feed, it falls more into the category of push.

RSS to the Rescue

RSS, acronym for (take your pick) Rich Site Summary or RDF Site Summary or Really Simple Syndication, began as an easy way for bloggers to track updates on blogs. RSS files are formed as XML files and are designed to provide content summaries of news, blogs, forums, or Web site content. Recently, RSS acquired the ability to transfer files and multimedia content, e.g., podcasts for videos, webcast archives, case studies, and similar.

Even if you have not used RSS, you may have seen those little "RSS" or "XML" buttons on your favorite Web sites or blogs. RSS is a defined standard with the purpose of delivering updates of Web-based content in the form of headlines and fresh content in a succinct manner. Users employ RSS readers and news aggregators to collect and monitor favorite feeds in one centralized program or location. Your feed is known as an RSS feed.

The consequences of spam have far-reaching effects. Everyone's e-mail box is clogged with spam. With antispam software that frequently does not make the fine distinction, good subscribed-to content is often filtered out and missed.

RSS, as a result, is fast becoming the vehicle that enables people to get good content of their choice and selection, and for lead generation, it provides the capability to link directly to customers and potential customers. Unlike with e-mail, the audience is in control. If your content is not of any interest to the individuals to whom you have directed it, your RSS feed can simply be removed from their RSS newsreaders. RSS opens up numerous new possibilities for lead nurturing and, on many fronts, for sharing relevant content with the audience on its terms.

When it comes to nurturing leads, your blog's RSS could become an invaluable tool. Assuming your potential customers have deemed your content to be relevant and timely and they have a desire to read its iterations, you have unfettered access to recipients who have added your feed to their readers.

The RSS feed means there is no e-mailing to do, no e-mail bounces, no spam laws or filters to worry about, just clean and easy communication having great flexibility. Marketers, for example, can offer an RSS feed that shares only your latest articles on a specific subject. Prospects and others whose interest in you may be limited to niche subject matter subscribe to your RSS feed, and their readers alert them each time you update the content for the niche subject they are interested in. Or you can offer special feeds on a regular and ongoing basis with pertinent information that reminds everyone why existing customers do business with you. Newsletter updates are facilitated quickly. The corporate Web site can provide a RSS feed for news and events that you feel will be of interest to a wide number of readers. It is even possible to set up internal RSS readers for employees to track trigger events affecting the company.

Blogs in concert with RSS can help generate public relations for your company. My blog has been syndicated by numerous online media outlets, and its posts are often treated as contributed articles. This has been great for increased traffic to our Web-site-heightened search viability and has positioned us as experts in the field of lead generation for the complex sale. Further, blogs by default provide RSS feeds, and many business-to-business firms have added RSS feeds to their Web sites. Thus, your news release content is directly accessible by the audience. The news media, also, like to stay current with companies of interest by subscribing to the appropriate RSS feeds.

As a new and evolving technology, RSS has early struggles with metrics and measurability. Undoubtedly, however, there will soon be tracking tools to aid in determining origin and destination of hits similar to Web site log files and e-mail tracking.

Some of the search tools to look at for RSS feeds are:

- Technorati—www.technorati.com
- Feedster—www.feedster.com
- Google Blog Search—http://blogsearch.google.com/

And Then There Is Podcasting

Podcasting derives its name from the iPod™ class of portable digital audio players that has taken the consumer market by storm. Podcasting is a method of publishing audio broadcasts via the Internet that allows users to subscribe to a RSS feed of new files. These are usually MP3s. Podcasting is increasingly popular due to automatic downloading of audio to portable players, personal computers, or any other MP3-compatible device for listening to at the subscriber's convenience. The term is perhaps misleading because neither podcasting nor listening to podcasts requires an iPod or similar portable music player. In a sense, it is like VCR or DVR for streamed media.

Though about as new as applicable technology can be, podcasting is by way of RSS feed and very easy to access. Major search engines and music sites have added the ability to search for podcasts and pull RSS feeds for updates. Podcasting is already successfully used for:

- Talk radio complete with topic and call-in listeners where voice mail boxes can play the audio into the podcast.
- Ideas or tips of the day.
- Short interviews with thought leaders and industry experts.
- Recording speeches or teleconferences for later distribution.

Podcasting doesn't necessarily require you to start from scratch. You likely already have high-value content that you produced for other lead generation venues, which will lend itself perfectly well to podcasting. Recorded webinars, webcasts, or teleseminars are especially good. Even articles could be repurposed into a radio show-like format analogous to books on tape.

A podcast I did with Anne Holland of MarketingSherpa on the subject of how marketers can improve Web site landing page conversion rates and attract more sales leads can be heard at http://blog.startwithalead.com/ weblog/2005/04/podcast_lead_ge.html.

Some other things to keep in mind if you decide to proceed with your first stab at podcasting:

- Know what you want to say and have a point of view.
- Be ready and willing to learn by trial and error because podcasting is still formative, leading-edge technology without a lot of helpful tools.
- Develop a working familiarity with sound editing software.
- Determine your comfort level with speaking in a broadcasting voice.

Not only can podcasting give your company and its image a new perspective, it can, in the realm of the spoken word, bring it an altogether new personality. And increasingly, as it evolves, podcasting offers the promise of being yet another highly effective way to reach and develop the potential customer.

New information and communications technologies spring onto the scene with breathtaking frequency, and it is quite likely that the search for the elusive qualified sales lead will continue to be enhanced by evolving technology. Although much of the early Internet hype has subsided, Web-based marketing communications more than ever play a crucial role in the modern-day business of lead generation.

Part Three

Lead Development for the Complex Sale

Chapter Sixteen

Working with Your Leads

In the end, no matter how cutting-edge your lead generation programs are, they still must come from a place of trust. Developing the prospect's trust is ultimately the best mode of lead generation. When there is trust, the high value your customers perceive is that you are there to be informative, and that leads to the clear understanding that doing business with your company would be exceedingly advantageous.

The complex sale scenario is not unlike that of a blockbuster movie. Untold creative blood, sweat, and tears are required before production even gets underway. A tremendous amount of money is spent before the product reaches market. Independent contractors and free agents, many of whom have never worked together before, are listed as principals. A big return on the investment is expected in a very short time.

As an investor without more than those few facts, you would probably turn away. That is, until you were hit with the sudden realization that, why, there is already a huge amount of equity here. Just what is the equity? It's in the names. Screenwriter, producer, director, actors. Theirs are names you know, that everyone knows. These are folks with proven track records. Their credibility precedes them and they are eminently bankable. How can we go wrong? Let's get the show on the road!

Like the movie, the complex sale asks that money be spent on something that will not manifest itself until delivered, implemented, installed, or otherwise put into motion. And it remains nothing more than a concept until a "yes" is consummated by way of a signed contract. Unfortunately, that is why a lot of lead generation strategies today end up in the scrap heap. And that is why a distinctively different way of approaching lead generation for the complex sale is required.

Equity in Working Together

Requiring a much greater degree of teamwork, the complex sale walks away from the once-accepted route of the sales department taking the lead from first contact to contract. Sales and marketing are so joined by purpose and process that there is, in fact, a common goal. The lead generation process, the marketing process, the sales process, and the prospect's buying process are interconnected by the collaboration of sales and marketing. Companies employing successful lead generation programs almost always have a dynamic marketing function that spearheads the program, which the sales team sells. Today, information technology—no longer a sleeper component but crucial to every business undertaking—joins the collaboration.

Think of this analogy. If sales and marketing were a manufacturing operation starting with raw materials—leads—and ending up with 5 to 20 percent in deliverable product—sales—it would soon be shut down to determine what is wrong. Companies, however, continue to spend untold dollars on lead generation efforts ultimately doomed to failure. The numerous business process improvement methodologies that have seeped into companies large and small for some reason are not yet as prevalent in the field of sales and marketing.

The traditional view of business process improvement is to remove unnecessary barriers, controls, and information silos between departments. Lead generation is quite another matter. Because much of the selling and buying occurs outside a controlled environment, more controls must be added to enable tracking progress. Lead management controls the process.

Lead management has the role of watching and directing the conversion of sales leads into customers. The "funnels" in Figure 16-1 representing the marketing and sales functions illustrate the lead management process, its components, and their interaction. The success of the marketing funnel directly impacts that of the sales funnel.

Breakdowns in the lead management process often occur when:

- Lead generation is viewed as a series of campaigns and not as an ongoing conversation.
- More leads are indiscriminately sought without properly managing those on hand.
- A single tactic is employed rather than a multimodal approach.
- Inquiries are improperly handed off to sales without due lead qualification.
- A lead nurturing program has not been implemented.

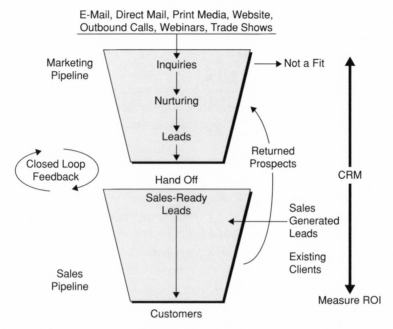

E-Mail, Direct Mail, Print Media, Website,
Outbound Calls, Webinars, Trade Shows

Marketing Pipeline

Inquiries → Not a Fit

Nurturing

Leads

Closed Loop Feedback

Returned Prospects

CRM

Hand Off

Sales-Ready Leads

Sales Generated Leads

Existing Clients

Sales Pipeline

Customers

Measure ROI

Figure 16-1 The lead management process

- Sales has not been given the means to hand unsuccessful leads back to marketing for further work.
- The database (CRM) is ineffectively utilized or poorly maintained.

Process mapping is a key component of improved lead management. As you map out your lead management process, the sales and marketing teams working together will identify each of the steps leads go through. The key question to answer during process mapping is who owns the lead at each step. There will be more on process mapping in Chapter 17.

Getting to Know You

According to a study by Cahners Reasearch, 76 percent of business-to-business customers report frustration with salespeople who don't understand their business.[1] A great leap of faith is asked of prospects who would put their job, their company, and their credibility on the line to do business with you, and in many cases they are not left with proof that you are capable of serving their

1 Susan Mulcahy, "Evaluating the Cost of Sales Calls in Business to Business Markets: A study of more than 23,000 businesses," (Washington: Cahners Research, January 2002), p 2.

needs. Seeking vendors with whom there is safety and comfort, they are on the contrary left to dread the things they fear most.

People caught up in the buying process have their own natural decision tree of how and where they are going to go in search of options. By building a dialogue with these searchers, you increase the odds that you will be one of the options selected. You also strengthen your odds with the level of contact you have with the potential client and the number of touch points you have successfully achieved.

Reaching the target with the appropriate message notwithstanding, marketers don't always have a good sense of the actual act of selling. For example, they may not be aware of when the salesperson is negotiating with a customer or potential customer. Or when proposals are delivered or presented. Or during conference confabs. Or by whatever opportunity there is to discuss the customer's needs squarely. Unless the marketer and the salesperson work together as partners, there is no way of sharing what is being discussed with the prospect or whether the message is getting through. Therefore, in attempt to make up for the unknown or the unexplored, many successful marketers profess that they consistently make conscious effort to put themselves in the customer's shoes, to think *like* the customer.

When we put ourselves in the shoes of our potential customer, we begin to understand why outsourcing companies are frequently viewed with suspicion. Jeff Tull in his book *The Prime Solution* argues that 75 percent of solution sales fail to deliver the results they promise.[2] Every new relationship, however, is fated at the outset to travel with a certain degree of fear, uncertainty, and doubt. Indisputably, potential customers will ask themselves:

- Is this company credible and solid?
- Is there a competitor of this company that is better?
- Will this company's solution really work for me?
- Can I afford this company's solution?
- Will buying from this company make a difference?
- Can I trust this company?

Remember that you are selling to people who, like all of us, have a store of negative experiences, and your goal is to break through these and ask them to believe in you. Meanwhile, they don't trust the hype. They are weary of pitches and all of the many manipulative sales and marketing methods they are exposed to every day. When they have a need, many deny that your help is required. Your motivations, as a result, obvious by your actions, had better

2 Jeff Thull, *The Prime Solution: Close the Value Gap, Increase Margins, and Win the Complex Sale*, (Chicago: Dearborn Financial Publishing Inc., 2005).

convey sincerity, honesty, and personal interest if you want them in your camp. Qualities like these along with the investment of persistent time and effort are what trust-building is all about.

Trust-building is also earning the prospects' respect to call on you when they have problems. If you have done your job, the potential customer should ultimately be able to conclude if not say to you directly: "You and I have been talking for quite a while. You give all appearances of understanding me, my company, and my industry. You provide useful and relevant ideas about the issue. You have helped me sell your solution to my colleagues, and they accept it. You are realistic in acknowledging that this is going to be a challenging project. I think you can do it, so let's get going."

Celebrated business-building consultant Andrew Neitlich says: "Companies want to work with companies they can trust. To do this, you need to show that you are the 'go-to company.' You have invested in the relationship and have educated your potential customers and existing customers?[3] He cites four criteria that he believes underlie trust—and therefore success in the lead generation process:

- **You are known.** There is awareness in the market of you and/or your company. Perhaps you have served the needs of similar firms. You have a proven track record.
- **You are credible.** You have a wonderful reputation. You are perceived as expert in your field. Others have recognized your abilities and contributions. Your dialogues with existing and prospective customers have been duly noted.
- **You are convincing that you can help.** You offer a plausible solution. Your track record shows that you have been there before. Open and honest communication are on-point and meaningful. You get it.
- **You are liked.** Your personal qualities stand you in good stead. You are not arrogant, pushy, or otherwise objectionable in your actions. You are considerate of and empathetic to my situation.

With these, all else being equal, you are the trusted advisor well on your way to making the complex sale.

Value by Sales Interaction

In the complex sale, the era of a single decision maker is over. There may be only one signature on the contract, but you can be sure that full buy-in came

3 Interview with Andrew Neitlich, President IT Business Builders, 5/5/2005.

from the buying team and sphere of influence before the contract was ever processed. The stakes in business have become too high for bad or misinformed buying decisions due to the narrow perspective or opinion of one person.

Bob Chatham in his article "The Customer Conversation" for *Forrester*® writes: "Firms struggle to overcome organizational and technical barriers that hinder customer connections. To dissolve these barriers, firms must create a new relationship strategy based on a conversation, not a campaign."[4]

Customers occupied in the buying process should feel that nothing is more important to you than their needs and wants, which the conversation must encourage and develop. Prospects' perceptions of your company and their ultimate preferences come from interaction with the sales team. Great effort must be made, therefore, to equip the sales team appropriately to perform its role in the sequence of events with relevancy and meaning, from contact to close.

Often there is an individual at the prospective firm who champions your company and its solution. It is incumbent that you foster this relationship to further the person's ability to sell your company's solution to peers in the prospect buying process. Providing the champion with information that could be used to overcome possible internal resistance and corral support for your product or service should not be minimized. A buyer's kit of literature pertinent to the business pursued and presented to your advocate is helpful towards that end. Without a champion, many complex sales efforts end up in oblivion.

Advance Potential Buyers with High-Value Content

Figure 16-2 illustrates that the various phases of the prospect's buying process entail individually diverse information requirements. Early on, research and information gathering are the predominant activities as a short list is made. Your goal at this initial stage is normally to strengthen awareness of what your company is all about and what you might have to offer under the circumstances. Pertinent tactics and data maintained at the ready will help illustrate and clarify. Content depends on the market and the particular needs and wants of the prospect but might include white papers, case studies, research reports, articles, etc. that directly reference or reflect a positive view

4 Bob Chatham et al., "The Customer Conversation," Forrester Research, Inc., June 2000.

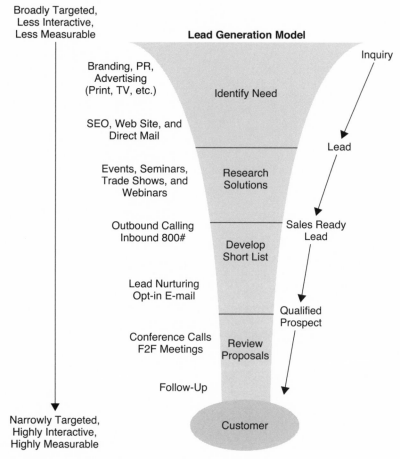

Figure 16-2 Information requirements by stage

of your company. And brochures as well? Not necessarily. The regular and ongoing quest of the sales team for more and more elaborate brochures often clouds the relationship-building objectives that are of greater priority in this pursuit.

Your willingness to persevere and pay unobstructed attention to detail are crucial to guiding the customer through the buying process—to the decision that you are indeed the right choice.

Chapter Seventeen

ROI Measurement and Metrics

Today it is no longer enough to know how many leads are being generated. In order to do their jobs, marketers are increasingly familiar with such things as lead conversion rates and the percentage of leads resulting in sales. Marketers are required to measure and report revenue and profits that are directly attributable to the lead generation program. This means having the ability to know the complete life cycle of a lead from initial contact to close.

CEOs obviously have an interest in where the dollars are being spent, especially when it comes to their marketing budgets. But try as they might, they have not been especially successful in pinpointing the actual contribution of revenue or profit from such marketing activities as lead generation. A concerted effort has been underway to remedy that, and marketers are finding themselves under increasing pressure to accurately measure and report their numbers. In fact, CMOs in more and more businesses are reported to be operating under the direct mandate to get busy reporting ROI and get that done *now*.

The degree to which sales and marketing are able to effectively collaborate is directly proportional to ROI, and that can be a major hindrance if the two groups aren't in alignment. Integration of the sales and marketing roles is crucial. Neither owns the lead generation process and neither by itself can make much of a statement as far as effective budgeting and spending are concerned. Nor does marketing influence the sales process per se other than to qualify the lead and hand it off to sales, from which point it has no control over the salesperson's ensuing efforts and the potential business that may exist. Nonetheless, despite perhaps not having the benefit of proper corporate mind-set, strategy, and tactics to make collaboration the integral part of the process that it must ultimately be, marketing frequently finds itself going it alone in the effort to generate, report, and justify ROI.

Lead management, the multiple-stage practice that manages the conversion of sales leads into customers, can give executive management a single line into all leads in the sales process for a true view of demand creation and lead generation performance. From it, everyone can obtain a clear assessment of marketing contribution to new sales. Lead management is in effect a sales-marketing bridge that connects the beginning and middle of the customer acquisition process. Without solid lead management practice, marketing ROI-based reporting will at best be a game of educated guesses.

In terms of actually measuring some aspects of lead generation—e.g., Web site, phone calling, e-mail campaigns, etc.—the data exists for all to see and is readily applicable. But exact measurement for other various, more obscure activities can be very soft or nearly impossible. The crucial focus for your lead management should be on those actions and results that can be tracked and measured as a basis for determining overall outcomes.

Measuring Lead Generation ROI

Measuring the return on investment from a lead generation program often proves to be less than an exact science. A great many outputs, including the most important, revenue, need to be measured with accuracy and consistency, and this is frequently in the face of shifting criteria and tactics. Inputs such as the cost of people, process, and infrastructure can be notoriously difficult to measure as well.

It is best to start with simple input and output measurements and get more complex from there. With planning and diligence, effectively tracking and measuring ROI are not only possible but play an important role in the overall lead generation plan. Some ways to look at this are the following:

The Big Picture

Big-picture concerns are addressed by, "How much am I putting in and what am I getting out?" The difference between the two is often expressed as a percentage, including, "What is the total cost of our lead generation program during a specific time period?" Such considerations as staff compensation, vendor and outsourcing remuneration, and building and materials costs are important.

And, "How much revenue can be directly attributed to leads coming from the program during a specific time period?"

The Details

Significant, too, is reflecting on the details when it comes to factoring ROI. ROI measurement can be the means of identifying the best—and by deduction, the worst—performing programs and tactics. For instance:

- How many qualified sales-ready leads have been put into the sales pipeline?
- How many qualified sales-ready leads have been put into the sales pipeline by lead source?
- What is the total cost by lead source?
- How many inquires were generated?
- How many inquiries were converted into qualified sales-ready leads?
- How many qualified sales-ready leads became closed deals?

With this kind of circumspect knowledge, the following are easily calculated:

- Cost per inquiry.
- Cost per lead.
- Cost per closed deal.
- Inquiry-to-lead conversion ratio.
- Lead-to-sales conversion ratio.
- Number of leads required to generate a single closed deal.

And an analysis comparing cost per qualified lead and per closed deal to:

- Cost per up-sell.
- Cost per cross-sell.
- Cost per renewal.
- Cost per reactivated customer.

Strategic ROI Analysis

Once you are comfortable with the process of measuring ROI and with sufficient data in hand, it is possible to ask more strategically oriented questions about ROI, such as:

- What would sales revenue look like without the lead generation program?
- How does the current period compare with previous financial periods?
- What sales percentage has come from leads created by the lead generation program?
- What percentage of forecast sales in the pipeline can be linked to lead generation activities?

- What is the value of the average program-generated sales opportunity compared to opportunities found by sales without the aid of lead generation activities?
- How have overall results improved compared to previous financial periods?
- Have sales cycles been reduced by lead generation activities?
- How many leads from the previous year are currently active in the sales forecast?
- What is the program cost expressed as a percentage of revenue contribution?

On the whole, it is generally accepted that the majority of marketers have regular and continuing difficulty tracking contacts through the lead generation process and the sales cycle. In fact, most are daunted by the often frustrating task of tracking leads and measuring ROI. The way out of this is by a process that includes:

- Sharing goals.
- Documenting the process.
- Providing sales the ability to return leads to marketing.
- Ensuring closed-loop feedback.

Let's examine each of these more carefully.

Sharing Goals

What gets measured gets done. Sooner or later, companies must come to grips with the issue of calculating return on marketing investment. And that goes nowhere until there is recognition that the opportunities can only be tracked by interaction among all of the principles. Metrics tracking, while not expensive, does require that each contingent in the process focuses on gathering data from its proprietary area of responsibility.

Technology does not create collaboration; it simply supports it. Costly and complex software is not the answer; one company recently abandoned its CRM because the sales team was flatly ignoring it. Instead, a simplified process was developed that would motivate the sales team to gather and report via a basic Excel system. Our sample reports here are based on that system.

Table 17-1 shows actual sales pipeline performance and reflects a situation where the firm's sales and marketing work closely together. Six-and-a-half percent of all leads were closed and 38 percent of proposals resulted in successful contracts. Without information like this, it would not have been possible to report that the lead generation program in play at the time generated 50-times ROI.

Table 17-1   Sales pipeline performance

Sales Process Stages	All Leads	% of All Leads	% of Leads Advancing
Leads–Hot, Warm, Cool	107		
Sales - Qualifying	70	65.4%	65.4%
Prospect	35	32.7%	50.0%
Profiled	25	23.4%	71.4%
Proposed	18	16.8%	72.0%
Active Contract	7	6.5%	38.9%

Table 17-2   Closed-loop feedback report

Current Lead Disposition

Status	Count	% of Leads
Active Contract	4	4%
Proposed	1	1%
Prospect	1	1%
Qualifying (Sales)	8	7%
Nurturing (Sales)	19	18%
Follow-Up (Marketing)	24	22%
Nurturing (Marketing)	1	1%
Qualifying	14	13%
Rejected (Marketing)	1	1%
Duplicate	1	1%
Lost Opportunity	1	1%
Not a fit	32	30%
Total	107	100%

It is important to know the status of every lead generated over any given period of time. Table 17-2 is an example of a closed-loop feedback report, again attributable to the sales department, and equally important to determining ROI.

Tracking and metrics must be ready to go when the lead generation program gets underway. From the standpoint of sales and marketing, the activities and performance of each must be measured by the same standards.

Documenting the Process

The fact that the quality of collaboration between sales and marketing directly impacts ROI unwraps the quandary that many organizations face, that their sales process is little more than the obscurity of a black box. No one but the sales team knows what goes on in that black box until a proposal or a sale comes along, and, of course, as much as 80 percent of the leads that go into the black box are rarely seen again.

I regularly encounter companies whose sales and marketing departments do not jointly agree on or understand their sales process. Nor do they have a good grasp of their potential customers' buying processes. As a result, it is particularly challenging for marketers at these companies who are trying to measure their revenue contribution and lead generation ROI. Process mapping, which is only beginning to be used in assessing sales and marketing contributions, can help.

Process mapping, a highly regarded procedure for creating a common vision and shared language for improving business results, is increasingly looked to as an essential step in measuring ROI. A company is a collection of processes, the business activities that generate value, customer service, and income. Managing these processes properly contributes to the company's success, and process mapping provides the method of focusing on those processes most important to lead generation and understanding how they work together. Table 17-3 is an example of a basic sales process that was mapped out in seven steps. Steps one through seven are from sales-ready lead to close. Process mapping is a well-known technique for creating a common vision and shared language for improving business results. However, this technique hasn't been widely adopted by sales and marketing.

Michael J. Webb, in writing on avoiding the common pitfalls of sale/buyer process mapping, says: "Leaders in both large and small sales organizations often make mistakes that undermine the potential of process mapping. A common result, for example, is that salespeople ignore the process and operate outside the system."[1]

1 Michael J. Webb, How to Avoid the Four Most Common Mistakes of Sales Process Mapping, Sales Performance Consultants, Inc., February 2003. <http://www.salesperformance.org/article_details.aspx?id=Mistakes>

Table 17-3 Sales process table

Step	Status	Description
0	FYI	Review requires special attention
1	Appointment	Lead qualified by marketing and sent to sales to be qualified
2	Qualifying	Salesperson is determining if lead is actually a viable prospect
3	Prospect	Salesperson actively pursuing
4	Profiled	Completed written proposal profile and opportunity assessment
5a	Preproposal	Confirming initial plan prior to formal proposal
5b	Proposed	Final proposal delivered
6	Committed	Agreement delivered and verbal yes to proposal
7	Active Contract	Agreement approved and signed
A	Nurturing	Was prospect and dropped out of the sales pipeline
B	Follow-up	Sent back to marketing for requalification, rescheduling, or lead nurturing
C	Rejected	This clearly wasn't a lead—returned to marketing
	Not a fit	Lead advanced beyond step 3 in sales process—salesperson decided not a fit

Webb cites four common mistakes that hinder success:

- Mapping all the details, losing track of the big picture.
- Focusing on the seller instead of the customer.
- Mapping the process without showing how the results will be measured.
- Buying somebody else's "ideal" sales process.

Webb goes on to say that the following principles can yield powerful results:

- Keep your goals in the foreground of your process map.
- Map tools, skills, and performance metrics along with the process.
- Engage your people in process mapping to define problems and solutions (must be cross-functional).
- Determine how to create value for the customer throughout the process.

As you map out your lead generation process, the sales and marketing teams working together will identify the steps that buyers go through during their buying process. The most important question to answer during process mapping is who owns the lead at each step. There can be shared responsibility, but only the marketing, lead generation, or sales team can own the lead. An individual must have responsibility for following up on the lead.

By process mapping, marketers are able to clearly examine each opportunity they identify and measure the effective rate of conversion at each stage.

Ultimately, process mapping can eliminate the blame-game because marketing and sales are together on the same side of the table.

It can also help prevent what I refer to as "The Sunshine Machine." This happens when you hear about overly optimistic or "sunny" individual sales forecasting that suddenly turns cloudy when the selling starts and must be adjusted to not adversely affect the accuracy of the sales plan. Suppressing the effects of the sunshine machine is often accomplished by little more than a few elemental steps that make the sales pipeline more realistic and in keeping with long-term growth and profit objectives. This sales management function might consist of:

- Soliciting individual revenue forecasts from the sales force.
- Consolidating the individual forecasts.
- Reducing the consolidated forecast by 20 percent.
- Reducing the revised consolidated forecast by another 20 percent after top sales management review.

The 20 percent is an arbitrary factor for this illustration only and would vary by case. The sought-after end-result is a sales forecast that would be more realistic in quantifying program planning and ROI.

Before the sunshine machine even comes over the horizon, however, effective management of the sales pipeline with a clearly defined sales methodology should be in place to enable more accurate sales forecasting. And this requires a good database for centrally accumulating customer and prospect data and the resources to collect quantitative and qualitative information with respect to new prospects. Also important is the ability to track both performance and effectiveness metrics and create a forecast based on field sales input and current and historical analysis of the sales pipeline.

Providing Sales the Ability
to Return Leads to Marketing

Handing off qualified leads from marketing to sales is like a relay race. Unfortunately, in this race, the baton seems to get dropped during the hand-off more often than not. And as in most competitive situations, the company that doesn't drop the baton wins.

The importance of a smooth hand-off—and follow-up—needs no further emphasis, especially in the face of the startling fact that 70-80 percent of sales-ready leads generated by marketing, amounting to billions of potential dollars, is never pursued by sales. Not only must the sales team be motivated to expend the required time to check out each and every lead, but also it must be quick to return the nonsuccessful leads to marketing to be put into the lead nurturing program. How well and how long it takes sales to respond to the qualified lead is directly influential on ROI.

Ensuring Closed-Loop Feedback

While measuring and showing the causative actions of marketing on tangible sales results will always be imprecise to a degree, the challenge is alleviated by employing closed-loop feedback. Closed-loop feedback—the principle of eliciting a continuous flow of pertinent information from the sales team—tracks each qualified lead from start to end, whether to sales close or to rejection. Though documented closed-loop feedback is most cost-efficiently and effectively generated by periodic input sessions conducted specifically for the purpose, it can be obtained individually from participating salespeople when necessary.

A typical closed-loop feedback meeting would include or address:

- Attendees.
  - Program manager and program expert (internal or outsourced).
  - Lead generation specialists (internal or outsourced).
  - Key corporate contact.
  - Sales team.
  - Interested observers.
- Reports.
  - Summary of month's activity.
  - Export of leads into sales stage.
- Agenda.
  - Status of leads in the sales process.

A software provider has a high-performance marketing team. The manager and his team get together with the sales team each week by conference call to close the loop on leads that have been created and handed over by marketing. The give-and-take covers everything from bottlenecks to new opportunities. It is a shared-learning experience that is very beneficial to both teams.

- Feedback on each lead if available.
- Leads active and moving forward.
- Inactive leads.
  - Incorrectly qualified?
  - Further follow-up?
- Leads for nurturing.
- Wins that can be celebrated.
- Things being done right.
- Things that can be improved.

The effective closed-loop feedback meeting is structured by the open discussion of all attendees generated by such questioning as:

- Have you been satisfied with the quantity of leads that has been generated?
- Are some salespeople getting too few leads?
- Should there be special focus on individual salespeople or industries?
- Do database record notes contain enough information to prepare for next steps?
- Are the notes clear and understandable?
- Are the notes a good reflection of what you hear when you call the prospect again?
- Are there other questions that would help you better prepare for the next action?
- Are current lead criteria adequate for qualifying prospects?
- Are there upcoming events that should be promoted when calling?
- How many calls does it take to reach the prospect?
- How many days after receiving the lead does follow-up begin?
- How many leads have turned into customers?
- What are the names of prospects that became customers?
- Is there anything unique about the leads that went into the sales pipeline or were closed?
- Are there prospects and/or customers that should be discussed specifically?

The expectation of full, dedicated cooperation of sales to provide meaningful closed-loop feedback sometimes defies probability. Often it is viewed as an explicit intrusion or at least a nagging inconvenience. A solution is to show honest interest in helping sell more in return for their sharing the results of their feedback. A little peer pressure can also be applied to advantage by virtue of your ability to actively track and report what each is doing and then compare it to the rest.

Companies that make this work have higher lead conversion rates than those that do not and ultimately improve all phases of the sales and marketing continuum and the return on investment.

Tracking ROI on Closed Sales

It has been said that most companies lose track of more than half of their leads somewhere in the sales cycle. In contrast to that, properly tracking ROI demands that you know where an opportunity falls at any given time in the sales process. Actually, it requires a working knowledge of the nominal status of every lead in the program.

Contact management software or CRM strategy is required to facilitate that, supported by a conversant staff and appropriate methods. And the sales team needs to perform within disciplined business rules that are not only followed scrupulously but also updated regularly. The responsibility for this is that of sales management, with distinct steps or microconversions that can be tracked from outset to close. Without it, measuring ROI on closed deals is difficult. See Figure 17-1.

This typical lead generation dashboard presents a company's vital marketing ROI metrics for its tactics in the organized and easily understood way that has made business dashboards so popular. In this case, the dashboard's greatest value would be in helping relate baseline ROI metrics to emerging trends and steering actions as a consequence of those trends. Major development concerns for this dashboard would key on getting to know the sales team's sales process, gaining close working familiarity with the universal lead definition, having sound means for closed-loop sales input, and ensuring data point accuracy. To remain true to their purpose, dashboards should be minimal in content and simple in format.

The CMO Council's Marketing Measures and Metrics Report says it best: "A survey of the nation's leading technology chief marketing officers reveals that the measurement of marketing performance and marketing return on investment is a high priority. Few companies—less than 20 percent—to date have developed meaningful, comprehensive measures and metrics for their marketing organizations. Over 80 percent of the companies surveyed expressed dissatisfaction with their ability to benchmark their marketing programs' business impact and value. Yet those companies

Total Marketing Budget $1,000,000

	Outbound Phone	E-mail	Website	Direct Mail	Seminars and Events	Advertising	Alliance Referrals	PR	Other Activities
% of Budget	30%	2%	5%	10%	15%	10%	5%	10%	13%
Budget	$300,000	$20,000	$50,000	$100,000	$150,000	$100,000	$50,000	$100,000	$130,000
Inquiries	N/A	500	500	500	500	500	500	500	500
Cost per Inquiry	N/A	$40	$100	$200	$300	$200	$100	$200	$260
% of Qualified Leads	N/A	5%	10%	5%	10%	5%	15%	5%	5%
Sales Ready Leads	250	25	50	25	50	25	75	25	25
Cost per Lead	$1,200	$800	$1,000	$4,000	$3,000	$4,000	$667	$4,000	$5,200
Close Rate	10%	10%	10%	10%	10%	10%	10%	10%	10%
Number of Sales	25	3	5	3	5	3	8	3	3
Cost per Sale	$12,000	$6,667	$10,000	$33,333	$30,000	$33,333	$6,250	$33,333	$43,333

Total Number of Sales	58
Average Size of Sale	$200,000
Total Revenue	$11,600,000
Total Marketing Return on Investment	1160%

Figure 17-1 Executive dashboard for lead generation ROI

that have established a formal, comprehensive measurement program achieve superior financial returns and have higher CEO confidence in the marketing function."[2] Hopefully, this will inspire you to manage your leads well.

2 "Measures and Metrics: The Marketing Performance Management Audit," CMO Council, June 9, 2004, p 3.

Chapter Eighteen

Lead Nurturing

The secret to successful lead generation—and ultimately in marketing in today's business-to-business space—is the underlying process of lead nurturing. Lead nurturing converts inquiries into qualified leads and starts the qualified leads on the trajectory to capture sales.

In general terms, lead generation initiates and perpetuates dialogue with the right people in the right companies in the quest for opportunities that are relatively imminent. Lead nurturing, on the other hand, keeps the conversation going over time, building solid relationships and allowing the creation of interest in products and/or services while bringing the leads to sales-ready status when the buying opportunity presents itself. The sales-ready state of such leads is the result of good lead nurturing and ultimately leads to better-qualified leads, higher close ratios, stronger sales pipeline, and shorter-than-average sale cycles.

Lead nurturing is the way to effectively follow up and turn any qualified leads into future sales opportunities by having consistent and meaningful dialogue with viable prospects regardless of their timing to buy. The basic objective of lead nurturing, therefore, is to keep in touch with the proper people at an appropriate level and on a regular basis. It is most certainly not about a salesperson calling every now and then to "touch base" and ask, "Are you ready to buy yet?" Instead, it is the act of maintaining mind share, building interest in what you have to offer, and developing trusted relationships with the people who can do you the most good. A company that has this kind of contact and quality communication with a customer or prospect will win that customer's loyalty for life. Lead nurturing is exceptionally effective in articulating your value proposition to maintain, in a subtle and consistent manner, a stream of the relevant information that is so important for the audience to know. This is especially true for the complex sale where patience and time to help prospects truly understand your value proposition are the norm.

Though a client's lead management program was working wonders, little thought had been given to putting a simultaneous lead nurturing program in place. When it was suddenly realized that 20 percent of the company's qualified leads were not being pursued by its sales team, there was no ready means for picking up the pieces. Research revealed that many of the leads were still quite viable and would likely assume an active buying stance within 12 months of their original inquiry.

A lead-nurturing pilot program was then installed. The first order of business was to contact these leads to determine where they were currently in their buying cycle. Criteria had been put in place to prioritize the leads based on their revenue potential, with the most recent given first attention. The plan was simple: Phone calling would be complemented by targeted relevant e-mail and several special offers. It began with a call to reestablish contact and to seek opt-in for the forthcoming e-mail series.

Within three months, 45 percent of these leads that had not been considered viable became sales-ready opportunities again. The firm captured an additional $1.2 million in sales as a result, more than enough to fund the lead nurturing program going forward.

The program was uncomplicated and easy to administer. It worked in large measure because the sales team was given the ability to hand back questionable leads to marketing for further development.

By staying in touch and continually conveying your message in anticipation of the day when the prospect is ready to buy, you are well positioned above the rest to make the sale. The frequent but discriminating communication afforded within this framework helps impart how focused you are on the prospect and its wants and needs and goals. And let's face it; it all still comes down to being in the right place at the right time, and ultimately it's better to have the strong relationship and brand awareness born of sound lead nurturing than not.

The overriding question, however, will forever be, is anyone in your organization formally identifying and following up with the potential future opportunities? You don't have to inquire too long to realize that few companies in the business-to-business arena still have no bona fide lead nurturing program—or even a recognized lead nurturing process—in place to bring the longer-term prospects along. Yet the potential for significantly increasing sales in a very cost-effective action is there for all to see.

What Is Lead Nurturing Worth to You?

The lack of a strong lead nurturing discipline can cost your organization substantial unrealized revenue. As mentioned throughout the book, research indicates that as many as 80 percent of leads are typically lost, ignored, or discarded. On the face of it, that borders on the untenable. But as startling as that may be, in context of potential sales revenue it is further shown that these disregarded leads can comprise upwards of 80 percent of missed sales!

Most legitimate inquiries don't lead to immediate purchases, but the inquirers eventually do buy. An in-depth study for Cahners Business Information of inquiries generated by ads and press releases in magazines serving the manufacturing marketplace found that six months after inquiring, 20 percent of the subjects had bought the product or service either from the promoter or a competitor and 15 percent said they would buy soon. An additional 65 percent indicated an interest and intention to buy in the future.

As Figure 18-1 shows, without lead nurturing in place to capture and cultivate early-stage leads, your marketing funnel misses valuable opportunities.

In contrast, lead nurturing stops viable leads from leaking out of your marketing funnel. As illustrated in Figure 18-2, lead nurturing widens your reach and recaptures opportunities that would have otherwise been missed. Consider starting a lead nurturing program with leads previously sent to sales where no action or progress has been made. Recycle these opportunities into the marketing funnel.

In today's commoditized business climate, the one thing that sets apart companies with a complex sale is how well their salespeople build and nurture long-term leads. It first must be recognized that selling by its very nature focuses

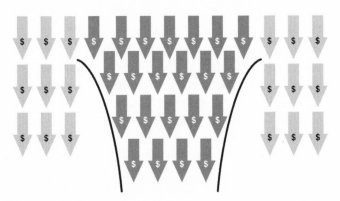

Figure 18-1   Without lead nurturing

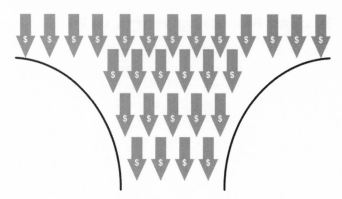

Figure 18-2 With lead nurturing

on short-term opportunities. Sales professionals, after all, are usually measured and paid on what they sell or deliver now. Under most circumstances, the sales team is either selling or performing prospecting activities. Little wonder, therefore, that they will ignore long-term leads if there is not a solid lead nurturing program in place. Marketing must enter the picture by going beyond the basic lead and helping the salespeople cultivate and develop the long-term opportunities that will sooner or later evolve into sales-ready leads.

So, the lesson is: Beware of unprocessed inquiries that are simply passed on to the sales group, be they reps, dealers, distributors, or whomever, for follow-up. You could well be leaving as many as 8 out of 10 sales prospects on the table for your competitors to grab off.

Brand Perception and Trusted Relationships

The expression "how you sell me is how you will serve me" is axiomatic wisdom that deserves to be top of mind when shaping a relationship. When you pay special attention to understanding a customer's needs and wants during the courting and buying process, it is insightfully obvious to prospects how they will be treated later. Lead nurturing sets the tone for how your prospect can expect to be dealt with going forward, to conclude that "this is the kind of company I want to do business with."

Regardless of what decision makers may have to say about it, there is another universal truth to keep top of mind: Buyers inevitably make decisions based on emotion and then backfill with logic. Successful lead nurturing identifies the prospects' needs and provides them with relevant, ongoing information that meets those needs with lead nurturing processes that build an emotional connection throughout the entire sales process. The salesperson in due course provides that emotional connection.

In spite of the fact that 70 percent of final customer brand perception and preference is determined through direct contact with the salesperson[1], today's economic buyers increasingly avoid talking with traditional salespeople if at all possible. They don't have the time nor do they trust salespeople as once was the case. They simply don't want to be sold, period. Instead, rather than from the mouth of the salesperson, they turn to information that is readily available on the Internet and through other sources to make their buying decisions. Reliance on these sources has caused the need for face-to-face contact to be delayed until later in the buying process. It has also diminished the value of face-to-face contact, and more is the pity.

When the time comes for an actual meeting, the salesperson must be recognized as a trusted advisor to be successful. "Trusted advisor" is actually a part of the company reputation or brand. The salesperson's role as trusted advisor is firmly established by way of the lead nurturing process. A recent study of business-to-business buyers shows that salespeople who do become trusted advisors are 69 percent more likely to come away with a sale.[2]

Because the complex sale requires that:

- Your prospect is familiar with you and your company and with what you and your company do.
- Your prospect perceives you and your company to be experts in the field.
- Your prospect believes that you and your company understand his or her specific issues and can solve them.
- Your prospect likes you and your company enough to want to work with you.

Trust becomes a key element for building and nurturing these suppositions.

Inspiring Trust

A crucial aspect of lead nurturing is the ability to provide valuable education and information to prospects up-front, on the way to establishing both the company and the salesperson especially as trusted advisor. By enlightening

1 "Bridging the Divide: Process, Technology, and the Marketing/Sales Interface," *Market Viewpoint*, Vol 15 No 4 (Boston: Aberdeen Group, October 2004), p 1.
2 Susan Mulcahy, "Evaluating the Cost of Sales Calls in Business to Business Markets: A study of more than 23,000 businesses," (Washington: Cahners Research, January 2002), p 15.

> Bob Chatham in his "The Customer Conversation" for *Forrester* writes: "Firms struggle to overcome organizational and technical barriers that hinder customer connections. To dissolve these barriers, firms must create a new relationship strategy based on a conversation, not a campaign."[3]

your prospects to the various ways your business fulfills their needs, you earn the distinction of being called an expert. Your salespeople don't sell and don't make pitches; instead, they provide insights and solutions, all within the realm of your expertise, and that is the reason they call you first when a need arises.

When your marketing program focuses on developing trust and confidence, time is freed up for more valuable pursuits. And as a trusted advisor, you will likely discover that you have the upper hand with your customer. No longer will you have to compete on price, the amount of selling required will be reduced, you will win more business on a sole-source basis, and more new business referrals will come your way. Above all, you will find yourself feeling awfully good about what you have to offer, as portrayed by the confident sales trusted advisor.

Think Like Your Customer

In every buyer's mind there exists a certain amount of fear, uncertainty, and doubt in the buying process. It goes with the territory. They are the customers of today who are weary of pitches, hype, pushy salespeople, and manipulative marketing. Potential customers could be mulling over questions like these about you right now:

- Is the company credible and solid?
- Are the people and the company trustworthy?
- Is there another resource that might be better?
- Will the solution really work?
- From a budget standpoint, is this affordable?
- Would this purchase make a difference?
- Will this be successful and is it worth doing?

A carefully crafted lead nurturing program can anticipate these and other questions your customers might have and respond to them with timely answers. And your answers serve as further reminder of how beneficial it

3 The Customer Conversation, June 2000, by Bob Chatham et al., Forrester Research, Inc.

would be to work with you. In effect, this inspires awareness that you are creating value by providing useful information.

Relevance is key. Lead nurturing is about sharing content that helps people find the answers to these questions and reminds them of the benefits of working with you. And don't lose sight of the fact that it is human nature to want to work with trusted advisors, those who truly "get it."

By consistently perceiving relevant content in context of your lead nurturing activities, your potential customer's inner dialogue will eventually be inclined to respond: "You and I have been talking for quite a while. You understand me, my company, and my industry. You have given me useful and pertinent ideas on this issue. You have helped me sell the idea to my colleagues and they understand and accept it. I realize this is going to be a challenging project, but I think you can do it. Let's get it going."

How Does Lead Nurturing Work?

A proven way to support the sales team's efforts and sustain your long-term lead nurturing process is to develop a program that reflects a defined process and is proactive, intentional, and actionable. The right program incorporates multimodal tactics designed to move prospects from awareness to interest to trial to action. It is not just a plan with dates and times and targets and tactics. Rather, it is a full-fledged program that is dynamic, integrated, and executed in a way that successfully aligns marketing endeavors with sales initiatives. The result is a purposeful undertaking that offers the greater probability that sales will adopt the working discipline of nurturing long-term leads.

When designing a lead nurturing program, ask yourself:

- Exactly who do I want to nurture?
- What problems does the prospect need to overcome each day?
- What is the prospect's top priority right now?
- Do I know what the prospect worries about?
- What messaging do I want to communicate?
- What is the best way to deliver the message?
- What action do I want the prospect to take?
- Will I need to demonstrate my product or service?
- If incentives or inducements are required, what are they?
- How often should I strive to be in contact?
- Which tools require direct sales involvement?

A lead nurturing program is not a single marketing campaign. Instead, it is a series of steps and communication tactics whose defined objectives are to develop and build a relationship with the potential customer—out of which will come conversations that convert to sales.

Typically, the lead nurturing program includes ongoing multimodal communication by mail, e-mail, or phone designed to provide the prospect with information to make decisions about your products or services. Depending on where the prospect is in its buying process, some tactics can be more effective than others. If a prospect, for example, is in the early stages of the buying process, it may be more receptive to information-rich tactics like how-to guides, white papers, brochures, or newsletters. As it moves further along the buying process, a webinar, demonstration, or checklist may be more appropriate. And when it is finally perceived to be ready to buy, there will be greater interest in meetings, needs assessments, or proposals.

The mix and selection of lead nurturing tactics should be based on what is being sold and how the specific market and prospect have been shown to prefer acquiring information. Alternative tactics are vast and varied, as evidenced by Figure 18-3.

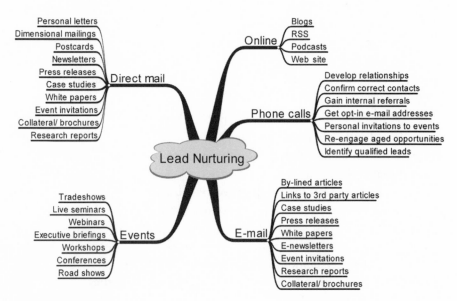

Figure 18-3 Lead generation tactics

Table 18-1

Plan A

Initial contact	Introductory phone call and follow-up e-mail.
Month 1	E-newsletter with voice mail alert to check.
Month 2	Recent customer success story via e-mail.
Month 3	Personal direct mail invitation from salesperson to forthcoming seminar with follow-up call.
Month 4	Case study and personalized transmittal letter.
Month 5	Recent Internet article of interest via e-mail with follow up call.
Month 6	Just touching base note via e-mail.
Month 7	Free report via direct mail with follow-up letter and call.
Month 8	Prospect calls you to become a qualified lead.

Table 18-2

Plan B

Initial contact	Introductory phone call and follow-up e-mail with brochure.
Month 1	White paper via e-mail.
Month 2	Article on useful application via e-mail.
Month 3	Article on pertinent technology via e-mail with follow-up call.
Month 4	Invitation to webcast via e-mail.
Month 5	Special offer for industry trade show via e-mail with follow-up call.
Month 6	Article on event ROI and online calculator via e-mail.
Month 7	Targeted campaign via direct mail with follow-up call.
Month 8	Prospect calls you to become a qualified lead.

The tactics employed and the frequency of touches will depend on the product or service being sold and the buying cycle of the prospect. A general rule is to bring salespeople into the process about six months before the targeted purchase time. Effective time lines might look like the ones in Tables 18-1 and 18-2.

Harvesting Leads

The database comes into play again as the centralized source for tracking each touch point and personal interaction in order to determine when leads are ready to be harvested, in other words to be handed over to sales. The hand-off is at the heart of the lead follow-up process and provides the ability to track interactions as the sales process continues towards the close.

What represents ideal timing at this point? Distribution of leads to sales is established in accordance with logistics for each salesperson and under ordinary circumstances should be completed by e-mail within 24 hours of the lead's becoming qualified. In those instances when the lead is deemed hot and necessary to be pursued immediately, the salesperson should be contacted by phone or other immediate means. It is very important that a staff person be assigned the responsibility of ensuring prompt and effective administration of the hand-off process.

The true value of lead nurturing comes from the disciplined technique of staying in touch with prospects while providing them with the "right" information as they move through the evaluation and buying processes. The end result is optimized mind share, efficient budget spending, profitable relationships, and increased business. Meanwhile, the competition is reeling over your new competitive advantage!

Proper lead nurturing programs open and strengthen sales pipelines and shorten sales cycles. They have been shown to yield anywhere from 15 to 200 percent in additional qualified leads, and sales close gains are even higher. One company calculated that nurtured prospects, which cited greater positive impression of the company when they became sales-ready leads, bought 100-250 percent more than those that were not nurtured but still bought.

Modern lead generation has come a long way. And though some will contend it has a way to go yet, the strides that lead generation has demonstrated in responding to today's business-to-business marketing challenges is nothing short of incredible. It is probably no stretch to say that well-formulated and closely adhered-to lead generation practice has been instrumental not only in the growth but the survival of many firms that are on solid footing today.

There is little question that companies engaged in the business-to-business or complex sale arena require a degree of sophistication in educating and nurturing customers and potential customers that on one hand is without precedent in the game of sales and marketing. On the other hand, certain basic underlying truths are present that quickly shoot down the notion that deep, radical change is at work here. After all, what's new about relationship building? At its basic level, lead generation is a commonsense approach to creating a business situation that merges human nature with modern-day communications and technological advances to reach those who are ultimately important to all of us, the customer and the potential customer.

My company is in the business of providing high-end teleprospecting and lead management services to organizations engaged in the complex sale, those that have determined that their lead generation requirements are immediate and in many cases crucial. Our experience is that first finding a way for sales and marketing to work together towards the common end— their collaboration so historically poor as to risk cliché—provides the catalyst that will bolster the strategic approach, whatever its structure. Still, we occasionally find ourselves so totally immersed in the client's business as we strategically identify, nurture, and deliver the leads that we have to step back and realize that the sales department, with qualified leads at the ready, ultimately has the role of making it all come to pass.

Selling is not for the meek, the timid, or the tentative, nor can it rely on the traveling salesman techniques that succeeded in yesterday's less-complicated marketplace. Improvisation may be great at a lunch meeting, but the complex sale requires a proven approach that depends on diligence and intelligence. Professionals like my group are committed to the long-term proposition that digging for leads, educating prospects, navigating the nuances of the complex sale, and creating new high-level ROI as a result is what has brought lead generation to the position it enjoys in the marketing hierarchy today.

Bibliography

Chapter 1

Byers, Nicola, "Holistic Marketing Should Not Be Holey," BizCommunity.com, July 2004.

Coe, John, "Why Is It So Tough to Sell Today?" Sales and Marketing Institute, 2004.

Dickie, Jim and Laurie Hayes, "The Sales & Marketing Excellence Challenge Study Results," CSO Insights, 2003.

Dickie, Jim and Barry Trailer, "Sales Effective Insights: The Top Ten Trends for 2004," CSO Insights, 2003.

Graham, John R., "Who's Responsible for Lead Generation?" *Selling*, June 1998, Vol 5 Issue 11, p 8.

Holland, Anne, "A Letter from MarketingSherpa's Publisher, Marketing Wisdom for 2005: 105 Marketers & Agencies Share Real-Life Tips," *Overture*, 2005, p 7.

LiBrizzi, Lorrie, "What Makes B-T-B Marketing Unique," *Business-to-Business Direct Marketing*, 1999, pp 30-31.

McConnell, Ben, and Jackie Huba, Creating *Customer Evangelists: How Loyal Customers Become a Volunteer Sales Force*, Dearborn Trade, 2002.

Mulcahy, Susan. Evaluating *the Cost of Sales Calls in Business to Business Markets: A Study of More than 23,000 Businesses*, (Washington: Cahners Research, January 2002), p 8.

O'Halloran, Patrick and Patrick Mosher, "Marketing: Underrated, Undervalued, and Unimportant?" *Accenture*, 2003.

Powell, Guy R. *Return on Marketing Investment*, RPI Press: February, 2003.

Sales Effectiveness: Helping Sales Sell, Boston: Aberdeen Group, June 2004, pp i-ii.

"SiriusDecisions 2005 Sales and Marketing Benchmarking Study," Southport, CT: SiriusDecisions 2005.

"The Value of and Accurate Database," Database Marketing Associates Inc, 2005. <http://www.b2bmarketing.com/resource_papers/Value%20of%20an%20accurate%20database.pdf>

Thull, Jeff, *The Prime Solution* : *Close the Value Gap, Increase Margins, and Win the Complex Sale*, Dearborn Financial Publishing Inc., 2005.

_____. *Mastering the Complex Sale: How to Compete and Win When the Stakes are High!* New York: Wiley, May 2003).

"Where Have All the Inquiries Gone?" Goldstein Group Communications Inc.

Chapter 2

Arnold, Catherine, "We Can All Just Get Along: Five Steps to Better Sales, Marketing Teamwork," *Marketing News*, American Marketing Association, 1 October 2004.

"Bridging the Divide: Process, Technology, and the Marketing/Sales Interface," *Market Viewpoint*, Vol 15 No 4. Boston: Aberdeen Group, October 2004, p 1.

Davis, Rick, "Sales 101: If You Approach Prospecting as a Disciplined Science, You Will Learn How to Work Smarter, Not Harder," Prosales, April 2004.

Dillon, Larry, "Dawn of the Lead Navigation Era: Fix the Missing Link Between Marketing and Sales," not yet published.

Donath, Bob, "Get Marketing, Sales on Same Wavelength," *Marketing News*, Vol 33 Issue 19, 13 September 1999, p 16.

Donath, Bob, "Three Steps to Marketing and Sales Teamwork," *Marketing News*, Vol 28 Issue 17, 15 August 1994, p 12.

"Gauging the Cost of What's Lost: Improve the Return on Resource Burn," CMO Council, November 2004, p 11.

Gilbert, Jennifer, "Sales and Marketing Management," *Marketing Management*, Vol 155 Issue 9, September 2003, p 16.

Gordon, Kim, "Team Effort," *Entrepreneur*, March 2004, pp 72, 76.

Interview with Pam Van Orden, President, White Canvas.

"Laying a Foundation," *The Loop*, Issue 6, 23 February 2005.

McIntosh, M. H., "Wish lists for B2B marketing and sales," <http://www.salesleadexperts.com/Wishlist.htm>.

Neitlich, Andrew, "Make That Sale…Without the Sleaze!," Sitepoint, 11 February 2004. <http://www.sitepoint.com/print/sale-sleaze>

"Sales Effectiveness: Helping Sales Sell," Boston: Aberdeen Group, June 2004, p ii.

"Sales Effectiveness: It's About Collaboration," *Perspective*, Boston: Aberdeen Group, August 2004.

Schmonsees, Bob, "Fixing the Marketing-Sales Disconnect," SandHill.com, 4 April 2005.

Stimpson, Jeff, "Developing a Marketing Culture," *Practical Accountant*, November 2002.

"The B-to-B Black Hole," R. J. Schmonsees & Assoc, 2005.

Viveiros, Beth Negus, "Bridging the Divide," *Direct*, 1 October 2004.

Watkins, Harry, "Getting Sales and Marketing on the Same Team," *B to B*, Vol 88 Issue 4, 13 March 2004, p 17.

Wemmers, Rick, "CEO: The Key to Fixing the Marketing/Sales Collaboration Problem," Ezine Articles, 26 January 2005.

Chapter 3

"2004 East Coast Lead Generation Summit Wrap-Up: Why You Should Never Classify Leads as Hot," MarketingSherpa.com, 24 October 2004, <http://www.marketingsherpa.com/sample.cfm?contentID= 2840>.

"Account-Based Marketing and Beyond: Next Steps in Demand Generation," ITSMA Commentary, 2004.

Babcock, Bill, "Five Common Lead Scoring Mistakes," BNJ Monthly eNews, Babcock & Jenkins Inc, 2004.

Coe, John, "Inquiries Are Not Leads!" *Target Marketing*, April 2002.

_____, The Fundamentals of Business-to-Business Sales & Marketing, (McGraw-Hill: August, 2003), p 15

Hitt, Justin, "Reasons Why Quality Leads Influence Your Customer Relationship Quality," *Inside Strategic Relations,* 2004.

Lambert, Jeanne, "Understanding the Difference Between an Inquiry and a Lead: The Key to Shortening Your Sales Cycle and Generating Revenue," Cerida Corporation, 25 May 01.

McIntosh, M. H., "How to Boost Your Company's Sales With Marketing," Mac McIntosh Incorporated, 2003, <http://www.salesleadexperts.com/BoostSalesWithMarketing.pdf>.

"Prospecting & Qualifying: Finding the Right Business in Today's Economy," *Short Takes*: Volume 2, Miller Heiman Inc, 2004.

Trailer, Barry, "Garbage In, Garbage…Well, You Know: You Can't Close Sales If You Don't Qualify Leads," *Sales and Field Force Automation*, January 1999, pp 35-36.

"Who Do You Want to Do Business With?" *Sell!ng*, Vol 5 Issue 11, June 1998, p 8.

Chapter 4

Athens, Debora, "Integration Between Marketing and Sales," MarketingPower.com, 2003.

Krol, Carol, "Marketers Face Obstacles, Reap Rewards When Segmenting Data," *B to B*, Vol 88 Issue 5, 5 May 2003, p 28.

Chapter 5

"10 Steps To Doubling Your Sales Without Any Costs," Townson & Alexander, September 2004.

Babcock, Bill, "Relevance," BNJ Monthly eNews, Babcock & Jenkins Inc, 2004.

Brock, Dave, "Is There Real Value in Your Value Proposition?" Partners In Excellence, 2003.

Cohan, Peter, "Death by Corporate Overview," MarketingProfs.com, 19 April 2005.

"Creating Business Value," Summit Group, 2005.

"High Performance: Why Marketing Needs to Change," BNJ Monthly eNews, Babcock & Jenkins Inc, 2004.

Holmes, Chet, "Increasing your Closing Ratio Three Fold, Designing the Ultimate Presentation," Jordan Productions, 2003.

Johnson, Landon, "Delivering a Value Proposition Is Not Enough: Companies Must Show Their Value Measurement," Viewpoint, DestinationCRM.com, 5 July 2005.

Konrath, Jill, *Selling to Big Companies*, Dearborn Trade Publishing, 2005.

Perla, Michael L, "What's Your Value Proposition," MarketingProfs.com, 1 July 2003.

"Outside-In: Prospect Personalization Techniques for Complex Products & Services," R. J. Schmonsees & Assoc, 2005.

"Quantifying Your Value Proposition," Gantry Group Newsletter, Issue 15, September 2002.

Rackham, Neil, "The Hunt for Growth: New Directions and Strategies for Selling," Strategy and Leadership, Vol 25 Issue 3, p 44. Republished with permission, Emerald Group Publishing Limited.

"Trigger Events for Sales Executives," The Cowan Group LLC, 2004.

"Value Mapping," R. J. Schmonsees & Assoc, 2005.

Zhivago, Kristin, *Rivers of Revenue: What To Do When the Money Stops Flowing*, (Jamestown, RI: Smokin' Donut Books, 2004), pp 107, 264-265.

Chapter 6

"50 Practical Ideas to Improve Your Marketing Efforts and Boost Leads," Vertexera Inc, 2002.

Harris, Joan, "8 Keys to B-to-B Success: A Guide to Reaching the Decision-Makers in Your Target Companies," *Target Marketing*, Vol 15 Issue 10, October 1992, p 40.

Jutkins, Ray, "13 Platinum Ways to Set Your Marketing Objectives," Baker's Dozen Collection, 2005.

_____, "Ready Aim Fire…Marketing by Objectives," Pertinent Information Ltd, 2005.

_____, "The 13 Most Important Questions to Answer as You Begin Every Marketing Program," Baker's Dozen Collection, 2005.

Kern, Russell "9 Tips to Improve Lead Generation," *Target Marketing*, Vol 25 Issue 10, October 2002, p 128.

McIntosh, M. H., "How to Use Your Marketing Dollars More Effectively in a Down Economy," Mac McIntosh Incorporated, 2002, <http://www.salesleadexperts.com/How_To_Use_Your_Marketing_Dollars.pdf>.

_____, "The New Business Needed Calculation," Mac McIntosh Incorporated, 2004, <http://www.salesleadexperts.com/newbusiness-needed.pdf>.

_____, "Free business-to-business (B2B) sales and marketing tools," (North Kingstown, RI: Mac McIntosh Incorporated, 2003), <http://www.salesleadexperts.com/tools>.

Perla, Michael, "What Revenue Should You Bet On?" MarketingProfs.com, 5 August 2003.

VanDen Heuvel, Dana, "Everything Stems From Expectations," Danavan.net, 11 April 2004. <http://www.danavan.net/weblog/archives/everything_stems_from_expectations.html>

Chapter 7

Hogan, Mary Kate, "Lead Generation Through Integrated Marketing Techniques," *Telemarketing*, Vol 12 Issue 5, November 1993, pp 18-20.

Interview with Cheryl Hatlevig, Director of Marketing, Adesso Systems.

Kranz, Jonathan, "Five B2B Copy Myths," MarketingProfs.com, 29 March 2005.

"Marketing Inspiration for 2003: Top Marketers Reveal Their Leanings," MarketingSherpa Inc, 2003.

Moreau, Robert J., "Maximize ROI Leads Using Three Media," *Marketing News*, 30 September 2002, p 18.

Mulcahy, Susan, Evaluating the Cost of Sales Calls in Business to Business Markets: A Study of More than 23,000 Businesses, Washington: Cahners Research, January 2002, p 8.

Robbins, Tony, "How to Get Any Business Going and Growing: Tony Robbins Interviews Jay Abraham," Abraham Publishing Group, 2003.

Chapter 8

"Accessing Senior Executives: Complex Sales Requires a 'Call High With Credibility or Go Home' Mentality," ExecutiveAccess, Wire The Market Inc., 2003.

Arnold, Terry, "Telemarketing Strategy," *Target Marketing*, Vol 25 Issue 1, January 2002, pp 47-48.

Chatterjee, Sharmila, "Bottleneck in the Implementation of Direct Marketing in the Industrial Context: Paradoxical Behaviour of Salespeople?," Institute for the Study of Business Markets, Pennsylvania State University, 1996.

_____. "Management Generated Leads: Panacea for Enhancing Sales Force Productivity?" Institute for the Study of Business Markets, Pennsylvania State University, 1996.

Davidson, Peter, "Cold Calling Tips," BeConnected, (BeTuitive, March 2005), <http://betuitive.blogs.com/beconnected/2005/03/>.

Fugere, Brian, Chelsea Hardaway, Jon Warshawsky, *Why Business People Speak Like Idiots: A Bullfighter's Guide,* (Simon and Schuster Free Press, March 2005), p 84.

Galper, Ari, "Cold Calling: The Reverse Selling Way," Reverse Selling Inc, 2002.

Gospe, Mary, "Building a Successful B2B Sales Development Organization," Bloofusion Inc, 2004

"Inside Selling: Selling More at Lower Cost," Stamford, CT: Gartner Inc., 1998.

Medved, Becky, "When It's O.K. to Cold Call," *Target Marketing*, Vol 21 Issue 3, March 1998, pp 77-79.

"Please . . .Return My Call: 50 Tips to Get Someone to Return You Call or to Get Past the Gatekeeper," Slife Sales Training Inc, 2003.

"Survey Results: If Your CEO Gave You $50,000, What Marketing Tactics Would You Spend It On?" Warren, RI: MarketingSherpa Inc., May 2004.

Chapter 9

Brown, Todd, "Free Reports = Increased Revenue: End Cold Calls by Getting Prospects to Come to You," Club Industry, April 2003, p 25.

"Eloqua Helps B-to-B Enterprises Increase Sales from In-House Prospect Lists, Web Traffic, and Web Seminars," Eloqua Corporation, 2 November 2004.

Galper, Ari, "How to 'Cold Call' Email," Ari Galper's Unlock the Game, 2004.

Godin, Seth, "Email Marketing," Nurture Articles, 1999.

"Lead Generation Top Tips: 12 Ways to Cultivate Leads with Email," LeadGenesys Inc, 2003.

"Lead Generation Top Tips: Real-Time Collaborative Prospecting: 10 Ways to Improve Your Telemarketing Results," LeadGenesys Inc, 2003.

McCraigh, Jim, "Using Email to Market to Top Level Executives and Decision Makers," *Direct Marketer's Digest*, 2003.

Chapter 10

Bauer, Elise, "Be A Thought Leader!" On the Job, 10 November 2003, <http://www.elise.com/web/a/be_a_thought_leader.php>.

"7 Guerilla-Publicity Tips for Businesses," MarketingSherpa Inc, 8 July 2003.

"Do Journalists Hate Your Online Press Room?" MarketingSherpa Inc., 21 August 2001.

Fireman, Jerry, "Painlessly Promote Your Most Exciting Success Stories," *Sell!ng*, June 2003, p 10.

French, Garrett, "Build Links and Your Brand: Article Marketing Delivers," Article Marketing, 23 January 2005.

"Graduating from Brand to Reputation," Perspectives, SiriusDecisions, March 2005 <http://www.siriusdecisions.com/newsletter/newsletter20/>

Habegger, Jay, *Taking Content Seriously as a Marketing Tool*, Boston: Bitpipe Inc, December 2004.

"How-To Articles Increase Responses and Track Results from Your Planted Articles," MarketingSherpa Inc, 7 November 2003.

"Launch Pad Survey on PR Perception Gap," (SHIFT Communications, 2004).

Lublin, Jill, Practical PR Workbook: An Easy-to-Use, Practical Guide to Develop Your Own Effective Public Relations Plan, Promising Press, 2002.

Markman, Steve, "Eight Steps to Getting Speaking Engagements," MarketingProfs.com, 28 October 2003.

McDermott, Billy, "A Report on Robert Bly's 'How to Become a Recognized Authority in Your Field," 2 July 2004.

Morris-Lee, James, "Database-Driven PR," *Target Marketing*, Vol 19 Issue 3, March 1996.

Rao, Srikumar S, "Case Study: Combining Three PR Tactics for Peak Impact," B2BMarketingBiz Newsletter, MarketingSherpa Inc, 17 June 2003.

Sewell, Howard J, "How to Write a Better Abstract," Tip o' the Month, Contact Direct, February 2005.

Shackleford, "Want Press? Become a Thought Leader," HealthLeaders News, 26 September 2003.

"Top 3 Online PR Mistakes B2B High Tech Companies Often Make," MarketingSherpa Inc, 1 May 2001.

"Top Seven Online PR Action Items for B2B Marketers," MarketingSherpa Inc, 11 December 2000.

Chapter 11

Cholewka, Kathleen, "What's Old is New Again," Sales and Marketing Management, New York, June 2002.

Duncan, George, "Making the Most of Trade Shows," *Direct Marketing*, Vol 54 Issue 1, May 2001, pp 35-40.

Granoff, Jeff, "A Great Webinar is NOT the Event: Go Beyond the Event to Really Succeed," *Marketing Watchdog Journal*, February 2005.

"Get Serious About Webinars," Bulldog Solutions, 2004.

"How to Produce Better Webinars for Fortune 500 Exec Prospects: 7 Tactics & 3 Worksheets," MarkingSherpa Inc, 1 December 2004.

Interview with Julia O'Connor, President, Trade Show Training, 5/5/2005.

Landlo, Michele, "Your Roadmap to Tradeshow Success," Skilset Communications Inc, 5 February 2002.

"Making Webinars Pay Enormous Dividends: A Process for Building Rewarding Relationships With Potential Customers," Bulldog Solutions, May 2004.

McIntosh, M. H., "Marketing Events: What Works, What Doesn't," MarketingSherpa Inc, 16 November 2004.

"Three Common Mistakes in Using Webinars for Lead Conversion," Bulldog Solutions, 2004.

"Using Webinars as an Effective Marketing and PR Tool," HRMarketer.com Blog, 11 January 2005.

Schultz, Mike and John Doerr, "Did Anybody Show? Seven Tips to Increase Attendance for Short Seminars," MarketingProfs.com, 2 March 2004.

Schuman, Evan, "What's Wrong With Today's Webcasts?" *B to B*, Vol 88 Issue 8, 14 July 2003, p 16.

Shefer, Daniel et al., "Webcasts as a Lead Generation Tool," Daniel Shefer, 2002.

Chapter 12

"5 Best Practices to Create a High-Impact Sales Lead Generating Web Site," MarketingSherpa Inc, 7 April 2004.

"5 Ways to Make Your Landing Pages Get Higher Conversions," MarketingSherpa Inc, 2 August 2004.

Buresh, Scott, "The Myth of Rankings: Beyond Search Optimization," MarketingProfs.com, 26 April 2005.

"Case Study: How Tweaking Site Design Increases Sales Leads," B2BMarketingBiz Newsletter, MarketingSherpa Inc, 10 June 2003.

Cates, Jeanette, "The Golden Website Handbook," Jeanette Cates, 2004.

"Day in the Life of C- Level Executives Part V," *Forbes*, September 2004.

Eisenberg, Jeffrey, "Persuasion Architecture: a Strategy to Map the Selling Process to the Buying Process," Persuasion Architecture Inc, 2004.

Gerrick, W. "Good Landing Page Design Tips," 1st Internet Marketing Solution, 13 November 2005. <http://www.1stinternetmarketing solution.com/article/design-a-good-landing-page.htm>

Hartzer, Bill, "The Business-to-Business (B2B) Sales Cycle," Corporate Website Marketing, 2005.

Holland, Anne, "Landing Page Handbook: How to Raise Conversions— Data & Design Guidelines," MarketingSherpa, February 2005.

"How to (Really) Gain Link Popularity: 5 Mistakes & 3 Proven Tactics," MarketingSherpa Inc, 26 April 2005.

"How to Combine Lead Generation, Search Engine Optimization, and PR in a Single Low-cost Campaign," MarketingSherpa Inc, 10 June 2004.

"Interactive Registration From Gets 300% More Completions Than Regular Sales Leads Forms," MarketingSherpa Inc, 31 March 2004.

Interview with Anne Holland, President, MarketingSherpa Inc., 11/08/2004, http://blog.startwithalead.com/weblog/podcast/index.html

Kostermans, Jeff, "How to Improve the Quality and Cost of B2B Leads," MarketingProfs.com, 2003.

"Landing Pages: Three Ways to Improve," Marketing Maven, GlobalSpec, Vol 1 Issue 6, 23 June 2005. <http://globalspec.com/mediakit/june05mmaven_landingpages.html>

McGovern, Gerry, "Eleven Search Engine Optimization Tips," MarketingProfs.com, 26 April 2005.

"Multiply Lead Gen Campaign Responses by Prepopulating Your Online Registration Forms," MarketingSherpa Inc, 3 March 2005.

Nguyen, Michael, "11 Ways to Improve Landing Pages," Digital Web Magazine, 25 May 2005.<http://digital-web.com/articles/11_ways_to_improve_landing_pages/>

"SEO: Do It Now! Search Engine Optimization Basics," HRmarketer.com, 5 October 2004.

Stoeckle, Grace A, "Limited Web Site Budget? Focus on Content," MarketingProfs.com, 19 April 2005.

"The DMA's State of the E-commerce Industry Report 2001-2002," Direct Marketing Association Inc, 2002.

"The SEO Industry: Gold Rush or Fool's Gold," HRmarketer.com, 28 April 2005.

Tangloa, Roland, "Search Engine Optimization and Other Web Site Myths Debunked," StreamLine, 18 May 2004.

"Welcome Messages Get Highest Open Rates of All Email Campaigns: How to Improve Yours," MarketingSherpa Inc, 9 December 2004.

Watlington, Mal, "Getting the 'R' In ROI From Web-Generated Leads," WebProNews, 29 November 2004, http://www.webpronews.com/ebusiness/ebusinesstactics/wpn-8-20041129GettingtheRinROIfromWebGeneratedLeads.html

Chapter 13

Bly, Robert, *The Lead Generation Handbook*, AMACOM, 1998.

Joiner, Harry, "Do Sales Letters Work," May 2005 <http://harryjoiner.typepad.com/proven_ways/2005/05/do_sales_letter.html>

Kern, Russell, "SURE Fire Creative Strategies," *Direct Marketing*, Vol 62 Issue 2, June 1999, pp 40-41.

Kranz, Jonathan, "Hmm, Hmm! Cooking Up Rib-Sticking Good Content," 800-CEO-READ Blog, 7 May 2005. <www.800ceoread.com/blog/archives/001155.html>

Kranz, Jonathan, "When in Rome, Do as the Romans Do," 800-CEO-READ Blog, 5 May 2005. <www.800ceoread.com/blog/archives/001153.html>

Logan, Jim, "Paper Direct Mail is Not Dead," JSLogan, 11 March 2005.

"Lead Generation Top Tips: 28 Ways to Optimize Direct Mail Design,"
LeadGenesys Inc, 2003.

Phelps, Russ, "Direct Postal Mail," Marketing Wisdom for 2005: 105
Marketers & Agencies Share Real-Life Tips, *Overture*, 2005,
pp 24-25.

"Successful Business-to-Business Direct-Mail Marketing," Sales
Management Report, Lawrence Ragan Communications Inc.

"When a Failing Company Hires You as Chief Marketing Officer:
Inspirational Turnaround Story," MarketingSherpa Inc, 29 October 2003.

Chapter 14

Cecil, Jim, "Customers in Crisis," Nurture Articles, 2004.

_____, "Nine Customer Love Letters," Nurture Articles, 2004.

Curry, Jay, "How to Make Money With Customer Interviews," 2004.

Graulich, David, "How Are You Doing? Ask Your Clients," Business
Horizons, September-October 1991.

"How to Get Fortune 500 Clients to Evangelize with Press, Analysts &
Sales Prospects on Your Behalf," B2BMarketingBiz Newsletter,
MarketingSherpa Inc, 1 April 2003.

Lewyn, Marc, "The Delicate Art of Generating Client Introductions,"
MarketingProfs.com, 21 October 2003.

Reichheld, Frederick R. "The One Number You Need to Grow," *Harvard
Business Review*, 1 Dec 2003.

Serling, Bob, "How to Get Industry Experts to Give You Hundreds of
High-Quality Referrals," B2BMarketingBiz Newsletter, MarketingSherpa
Inc, 9 October 2002.

Chapter 15

Burns, Fergus, "Top 5 Reasons to Use RSS," MarketingProfs.com, 12 April
2005.

Bruner, Rick, "Business Blog Consulting," March 2005, <http://www.businessblogconsulting.com/2005/03/percentage_of_f.html>.

Chisholm, Kari, "Blogging 10," Politics and Technology, 30 December 2004. <http://www.politicsandtechnology.com/2004/12/blogging_101.html>

Dysart, Joe, "RSS Gives Marketers Uncensored Channel," DM News, 27 April 2005.

Flitter, Bill, "A Sound Case to Include Blogs and RSS in Your Marketing Mix," Pheedo, 6 March 2005. <http://www.pheedo.info/archives/000250.html>

Hrastnik, Rok, "The Business Case for RSS," MarketingStudies.net, 2005.

Mulcahy, Susan. "Evaluating the Cost of Sales Calls in Business to Business Markets: A Study of More than 23,000 Businesses," Cahners Research, January 2002, p 15.

Richmond, Riva "Blogs Keep Internet Customers Coming Back," Wall Street Journal Online, March 2005. Copyright 2005 by Dow Jones & Co Inc, Reproduced with permission of Copyright Clearance Center.

Spencer, Stephan, "Move Over Blogs: Here Come Podcasts," MarketingProfs.com, 22 March 2005.

Teten, David and Scott Allen, *The Virtual Handshake*, AMACOM, 2005.

Tsuruoka, Doug, "Blogs Bring a Boost to Jupiter Research," *Investors Business Daily*, 2 November 2004.

VanDen Heuvel, Dana, "Dear Company, I Want a Relationship with You. Please Send RSS Feed or E-mail Newsletter," Danavan.net, 6 May 2005. <http://www.danavan.net/weblog/archives/cat_rss.html>

Wright, Jeremy, "Ensight," March 2005 <http://www.ensight.org/archives/2005/03/07/how-many-fortune-500s-blogging/>.

Chapter 16

Interview with Andrew Neitlich, President IT Business Builders, 5/5/2005.

Mulcahy, Susan, "Evaluating the Cost of Sales Calls in Business to Business Markets: A study of more than 23,000 businesses," (Washington: Cahners Research, January 2002), p 2

Neitlich, Andrew, "A Revolutionary Marketing Strategy...Trust Me," Sitepoint, 21 November 2003. <http://www.sitepoint.com/print/marketing-strategy-trust>

"The Customer Conversation", June 2000, by Bob Chatham et al., Forrester Research, Inc.

Thull, Jeff "The Prime Solution: Close the Value Gap, Increase Margins, and Win the Complex Sale," Kaplan Publishing, January 2005, p xviii.

Trumfio, Ginger, "Sales Secrets to Take to the Grave," Sales & Marketing Management, Vol 146 Issue 1, January 1994, p 57.

Chapter 17

Bannan, Karen J., "Connecting E-mail to your CRM System: Integrating E-mail Data Can Yield Big Results, But It's Not Always an Easy Task," *B to B*, 17 January 2005.

Berkowitz, Jim, "State of the Art lead Tracking," Jim Berkowitz's e-Journal, CRM Mastery Inc, 2 February 2005. <www.crmmastery.com/weblog/2005/02/02.html>

Budds, Niall, "Shared Goals Foster Better Lead Management," *Marketing News*, 1 October 2004, pp 17-18.

Decker, Sam, "10 Clues You Have a Marketing ROI Culture," Decker Marketing, 26 April 2005.

Donaldson, Tim, "Measure Returns With Process Integration," *Marketing News*, 1 March 2004, p 23.

Eidson, Sam, "Program Effectiveness Relies on Infrastructure," *Marketing News*, 1 October 2004, pp 16, 18.

Friedman, Mark, "All Sales Inquiries Are Important...It's Just That Some Are More Important Than Others," Cerius Consulting, 2005.

"Measures and Metrics: The Marketing Performance Management Audit," CMO Council, June 9, 2004, p 3.

Michael J. Webb, "How to Avoid the Four Most Common Mistakes of Sales Process Mapping", Sales Performance Consultants, Inc., February 2003, http://www.salesperformance.org/article_details.aspx?id=Mistakes

"Process and Organizational Best Practices for Pipeline Management," Seibel Systems, 2005.

"Relentless Lead Qualification: How to Do It & How to Track Results Properly," MarketingSherpa Inc, 29 September 2004.

Roffman, Sally, "Leading the Way! How to Create an Integrated, Brand-Savvy Lead Generation Campaign," *Triangle TechJournal*, 2005.

Stevens, Ruth P, "Linking the Marketing-Sales Loop," Gale Group, April 2000.

"Your Sales Opportunity Pipeline Still Needs to be Managed," Defying the Limits, Montgomery Research, 2005, pp 6-7.

Chapter 18

"Bridging the Divide: Process, Technology, and the Marketing/Sales Interface," *Market Viewpoint*, Vol 15 No 4 Boston: Aberdeen Group, October 2004, p 1.

"Contact to Contact: An Improved Sales Paradigm," Aberdeen Group, 2001.

Canada, Henry, "Managing Abundance: How to Manage the Leads That Will Flood the Marketplace in 2005," *Source Book 2005, Selling Power*, 2005, pp 30-32.

Carroll, Brian, "Lead Nurturing: Picking the Right Bananas," InTouch Inc, February 2004. <http://www.increasemysales.com/article.asp?ARTI-CLEID=162>

Coleman, Chris, "The Green Banana Papers : Marketing Secrets for Technology Entrepreneurs," Decatur, GA: St. Barthelemy Press, 2003.

Ellison, Carol, "Cultivating a Loyal Following: One Strategy is to Nurture Client Relationships," Var Business, CMP, 4 October 2004.

"Gain Control with Cultivation," BNJ Monthly eNews, Babcock & Jenkins Inc, 2004.

Gandia, Ed, "Maximizing Your Lead Generation Efforts by 'Recycling' Your Leads," Ezine Articles, 17 December 2004.

Griggs, Robyn, "Give Us Leads! Give Us Leads!" Sales and Marketing Management, Vol 149 Issue 7, July 1997, pp 66-70.

Mulcahy, Susan *Report #210.0.* Washington: Cahners Research, January 1992.

_____"Evaluating the Cost of Sales Calls in Business to Business Markets: A Study of More than 23,000 Businesses," Washington: Cahners Research, January 2002, p 15.

Mednick, Barbara K, "Successfully Managing Sales Leads," *Star Tribune*, 29 September 2003.

Ramsey, Steven B et al., "Timing the Handoff," Accenture, 2003.

"Real-Life Story: Sales & Marketing One Happy Family & 100% of Leads Followed Up On," MarketingSherpa Inc, 17 February 2005.

Wease, Greg, "Lead Qualification and Management," MarketingPower.com, 2004.

Index

About the Author

Brian J. Carroll is founder and CEO of InTouch Inc., one of the first companies to provide lead generation solutions for the complex sale and recognized by *Inc.* magazine as one of America's fastest growing companies. He speaks to 20,000 people a year on improving sales effectiveness and lead generation strategies. Carroll has been featured in publications including *The Wall Street Transcript, Sales and Marketing Management,* and *Inc.* His blog, http://blog.startwithalead.com, is read by thousands each week.

InTouch can be contacted at:
E-mail: info@leadgenerationbook.com
B2B Lead Generation Blog: http://blog.startwithalead.com
Book Web site: http://leadgenerationbook.com
InTouch Web site: http://www.startwithalead.com